"Nancy has written a great book that will help young women identify who they are—and how much they are loved! She's a sojourner who can give you a valuable roadmap and encouragement for your journey."

Becky Tirabassi
Change Your Life, Inc.

"Nancy Wilson has done it again—she tenderly ministers to women who struggle with their identity. This is a warm, thoughtful book that will encourage many."

Dennis & Barbara Rainey
FamilyLife

"I have known Nancy for many years. She is a woman who has a passion and love for Jesus Christ and teenagers. She has written a book that every teen needs to read for their sake and for the sake of their friends who are going through similar struggles. It is timely, insightful, practical, and needed for today. I highly recommend it!"

Rev. Greg Speck, Youth Specialist
Royal Servants International, Reign Ministries

"Knowing Nancy today, it's hard to believe she ever struggled with an eating disorder. She is proof that very destructive habits can cease and that individuals can truly be set free. My prayer is that this book will wind up in the hands—then hearts—of young women who, like Nancy, have bought the lie that personal value can be had by cutting corners—and apart from Christ."

Robert S. Waliszewski
Youth Culture Specialist, Writer, Speaker

"Nancy is absolutely the most inspiring, vivacious, encouraging person I've ever met! Her overflowing love for God and His people has bubbled effectively onto the pages of this much-needed book."

Dr. Joe White, President
Kanakuk Kamps

"Nancy's book is a straightforward, hard-hitting revelation of what can happen to a person lured by society's view of perfection. Her heart-rending story has the potential to help those caught in the trap of pursuing the world's ideals. Teenagers, young adults, and parents will find this must reading."

Vonette Z. Bright, Co-founder
Campus Crusade for Christ

"Jesus came to set captives free, yet many of God's precious children are agonizing in the bondage of eating disorders. Nancy has written a long-needed book full of hope, birthed out of her own journey from slavery to freedom in Christ."

Rich Miller
Freedom in Christ Ministries

"This book will captivate you as it reveals God's healing unconditional love. It reaches into the hearts of those struggling with the emotional and physical trauma of an eating disorder, offering hope to parents and young people alike. As a nutrition consultant, working for 20 years with individuals who suffer from eating disorders, I highly recommend *In Pursuit of the Ideal*."

Joan Gangwer, MS, RD, CDE
Nutrition Consultant

"Through rich personal stories, poetry, and Scripture, Nancy captures the core of our desires, dreams, and needs as women and shows us that regardless of the depth of our struggles or sins, God can transform us from an ugly caterpillar to a beautiful butterfly."

Karen Covell, TV Producer
Director, The Hollywood Prayer Network

"In a story full of warmth, honesty, and humor, Nancy takes you inside her heart on her quest for love and acceptance until she finds what she's seeking. In a time when perfect media images define the norm, Nancy will introduce you to one who accepts you as you are."

Andrea Buczynski
Global Campus Ministry Team

iN PURSUiT of the iDEAL

FiNDiNG YOUR iDENTiTY AND LiViNG iN TRUE FREEDOM

NANCY M. WiLSON

NewLife
PUBLICATIONS

In Pursuit of the Ideal:
Finding Your Identity and Living in True Freedom

Published by
NewLife Publications
A ministry of Campus Crusade for Christ
P.O. Box 620877
Orlando, FL 32862-0877

Design and production by Genesis Group

Cover by Larry Smith & Associates

Printed in the United States of America

ISBN 1-56399-210-8

Unless otherwise indicated, Scripture quotations are from the *New International Version*, © 1973, 1978, 1984 by the International Bible Society. Published by Zondervan Bible Publishers, Grand Rapids, Michigan.

Scripture quotations designated NLT are from the *New Living Translation*, © 1996 by Tyndale House Charitable Trust.

Scripture quotations designated TLB are from *The Living Bible*, © 1971 by Tyndale House Publishers, Wheaton, Illinois.

Scripture quotations designated NASB are from the *New American Standard Bible*, © 1960, 1962, 1963, 1968, 1971, 1972, 1973, 1975, 1977 by the Lockman Foundation, La Habra, California.

Scripture quotations designated *The Message* are taken from *The Message*, © 1993, 1994, 1995, 1996, 2000, 2001, 2002. Used by permission of NavPress Publishing Group.

For more information, write:

Campus Crusade for Christ International—100 Lake Hart Drive, Orlando, FL 32832, USA

L.I.F.E., Campus Crusade for Christ—P.O. Box 40, Flemington Markets, 2129, Australia

Campus Crusade for Christ of Canada—20385 69th Avenue, Langley, BC, V2Y 1N5, Canada

Campus Crusade for Christ—Fairgate House, King's Road, Tyseley, Birmingham, B11 AA, United Kingdom

Lay Institute for Evangelism, Campus Crusade for Christ—P.O. Box 8786, Auckland, 1035, New Zealand

Campus Crusade for Christ—9 Lock Road #3-03, PacCan Centre, Singapore

Great Commission Movement of Nigeria—P.O. Box 500, Jos, Plateau State, Nigeria, West Africa

I dedicate this book to my earthly father and my heavenly Father. Dad, thanks for becoming a source of the unconditional love that flows from God's heart. And to my nieces Amy, Ashley, Allyssa, Jessica, and Emily, whom I love and treasure. You represent the next generation of young women. May you be blessed by these truths.

"How precious to me are your thoughts, O God!"

PSALM 139:17

CONTENTS

ACKNOWLEDGMENTS

My thanks and appreciation to…

Michelle Treiber and John Nill at New*Life* Publications, for believing in me and this project. You have been a blessing and encouragement to me.

Tammy Campbell, my wonderful and gifted editor. Wow! You are amazing and you made this process fun. Your insights and hard work have been invaluable.

Lynn Copeland, whose tremendous gift of editing, helping the manuscript to flow with clarity, has been so appreciated.

Lisa Thompson, my precious friend who catapulted this project forward with her tireless typing and laying out the manuscript until the wee hours. What an answer to prayer you are!

Josh and Dottie McDowell, for your sacrificial help in the midst of preparing for Katie's wedding. What true friends you are!

Kelly Bauer, your compassionate heart for healing broken lives helped me in my writing. Thank you for your wise and practical contribution to the book.

Dan and Pat Lee, what faithful friends and servants you are to help me when I most needed you. I'm very grateful.

Greg Speck, for his friendship and valuable critique in communicating effectively. Your insights were tremendous and your heart for young people has inspired me.

Andrea Buczynski, Kirsten Vienneau, Donna Nuss, Joan Gangwer, Melanie Wilson, Dawn Angelich—dear friends who gave helpful counsel and advice.

Christi Mansfield, who creatively worked with me to get this project started.

Marian Drops, my dear friend who has continually been my prayer partner, encouraging me to tell my story. I love you!

Peggy and David Noe and my friends at Canaan in the Desert and God's Place, for providing beautiful, inspirational surroundings in which I could write.

Marcie Northrup, who introduced me to a personal relationship with Jesus Christ, and Brenda Mobley, who helped me grow in this awesome new relationship.

My family, who lived through the journey with me and have continually provided a safe haven of love and acceptance. Thank you for being there for me.

My mother, who has always been and will remain my constant inspiration. Mom, you will receive your full reward in heaven!

My heavenly Father, who sent His Son Jesus to heal, deliver, and restore me to wholeness. I love and praise You always!

FOREWORD

Tackling a topic like the one in this book is not easy. Our culture continues to ravage one's sense of self-worth, causing many young men and women to consider extreme measures to protect or enhance their self-image. Nancy has spoken to this very crucial issue. Not only does she address some of the pressures with which young people are bombarded, she also tells her story so effectively through honesty and vulnerability. She shares, on a heart level, her painful search for worth and value which led her to a serious eating disorder.

As parents whose hearts beat for the next generation of young people, too often we see the anguish of young men and women grappling with these issues. This book offers great insight into the minds of young people and uncovers the tremendous need for parents to help shape their children's sense of identity and self-worth. Dads, you have a critical role in your daughters' lives. Nancy will enlighten you to the significance of it. Moms, the impact of your model and affirmation are enormous!

But what about young people who don't have these role models? There is hope for them as well. Nancy brings you to the point of discovering solutions that literally changed her life and rescued her out of a pit of incredibly destructive behavior. We highly recommend this book and encourage you to take this journey with Nancy.

In Pursuit of the Ideal will lead you to pursue the One who is ideal. He can offer life changes and a new foundation from which to build your identity. We love Nancy and are proud of this book that she has written to meet a significant need of this generation. Women of all ages will be blessed by this book. Parents will discover ways to encourage their children and to point them in the right direction. Expect Nancy's story to challenge you and give you hope!

JOSH AND DOTTIE MCDOWELL

iNTRODUCTiON

The lights were turned low and candles were lit; eight guys and gals formed a circle in my friend's basement. The bottle was spun...my heart started to beat faster...my palms grew sweaty. Would it stop at me? The choice was risky: either divulge the truth or take a dare. What would they ask?

No telling what they would demand to know about my love life, deep feelings, or secrets never told. But the alternative was equally scary. They could dare me to do something I didn't want to do: make out with somebody, take off some clothes...my imagination went wild. What would I choose?

It may be safer to tell the truth—or would it? To be real can be risky. What would my friends think if I really shared the "inside scoop"? Would I be embarrassed? But dare I give control to the wild imagination of my friends?

Oh, it's only a game. What do I have to lose? I reasoned. "I'll take a dare!" I told the group.

In reality, life can be like this. The choice before us is to be authentic and real, or to dare to go along with the crowd, more concerned with keeping our image. The scary part is when we don't know who we are or the truth is too painful to face. We may opt for daring to do and be what everyone else wants us to, never discovering our true identity.

What image do you strive to live up to? Imagine your "ideal life." What would it be like? I dreamed of an exciting, adventurous, "on the edge" life filled with significance and purpose.

Have you ever felt this way? In your mind's eye, you can envision this ideal life, but the reality is far different. Perhaps life has given you some challenges to overcome, disappointments to face, hurts to survive, or a hope that needs to be restored.

The depressing "bad hair day" is often a symptom of a "very bad heart day." Maybe like me, you've tried to put on a happy face and keep up an ideal image, all the while wishing you had a different body, the perfect boyfriend or husband—essentially the "new and improved life" that would make everything better. Whatever your secret longing, it may lead you to pursue satisfaction in destructive ways as I did, rather than deal with reality. See if you can identify with my experience.

Go back with me to one night at a high school dance. I had my heart set on attracting the attention of my former boyfriend, whom I still cared for. As usual, I was having a great time laughing with friends and was in the center of the action. But then I noticed my ex-boyfriend flirting with another girl. That hurt! He even started to dance with her. The next thing I knew, he spent the rest of the evening with her!

Devastated, I ran into the bathroom with my girlfriend and began to cry. The illusion of this ideal relationship came crashing in on me. As I sobbed there in the bathroom, I felt something more—an issue deep in my heart. I felt a longing to be loved, accepted, and valued.

You see, I seemed to have it all together on the outside, like a package wrapped neatly with a nice bow. After all, wasn't this the ideal: being popular, having great relationships with my girlfriends and cool boyfriends, pleasing my parents and God, and feeling that my life was making a difference? As long as things went according to my standards, life was great.

Even when I was disappointed or sad, I hid my true emotions by putting on a happy face. But on the night of the dance, I broke down. When I got home, I grabbed a box of cookies and turned on the TV. To numb the pain in my heart, I ate cookie after cookie, faster and faster, until I finished the whole box. I could hardly believe it! As soon as my stomach began to feel full and bloated, I was soaked in shame and regret.

All I could think about was how the huge number of calories I'd consumed would affect my weight. I dealt with the calorie problem in the way that would least disrupt my life: I went to the bathroom and made myself sick. This marked the beginning of my long struggle. Little did I realize that bingeing would become a way to cope with my emotions without dealing with the issues of my heart. My goal was to keep up my image while suppressing any uncomfortable feelings.

As a teenager, my search for the ideal image—body, boyfriend, and life—practically consumed me. Although I was in pursuit of the ideal, I didn't know who I really was. I just knew what I thought would make me accepted, valued, wanted, and loved. I dared to take the risk!

This search for identity and purpose often defines the teen years. Most girls spend great amounts of time imagining what their ideal life would be like, which leads to their preoccupation with models, magazines, and music groups.

The search can be beneficial if they let the right people and resources influence them. However, with the wrong influences, it can also be devastating and can continue to control their life way beyond the teen years.

People throughout the centuries have struggled with questions of identity and purpose in life. In recent years, the result of some of these struggles has been brought out in the open. Specifically, eating disorders and other addictive behaviors have become more widely known in the last twenty years or so. How did we get to this point? Think about what the world was like only one hundred years ago. Imagine newly discovered electricity, ice cream parlors, bicycles built for two, horse-drawn carriages, newspapers, a handful of magazines, and the crank telephone. It was a world without airplanes, cars, radios, televisions, microwaves, computers, CD players, VCRs, palm pilots, or cell phones. Just think of it—no media as we know it today! It's almost unimaginable!

Even as late as 1951, most people still rode trains. Few families had more than one car, and commercial flying was not a common practice. Nearly everyone listened to the radio, though the television age was dawning. Women admired the attractive models pictured in magazines, but were not consumed with the thought of becoming models themselves.

In 1959 Barbie was born, and Cinderella was about to capture every young girl's heart. Prince Charming also entered their dreams and fantasies.

From the 1960s on, TV and magazine images set the standard for the ideal American woman. Take a brief look at the top models of each decade. The 1960s had "stick thin" Twiggy. The 1970s had "big girl" Cheryl Tiegs. The 1980s had "healthy girl" Cindy Crawford. The 1990s reverted back to the stick-thin look with emaciated Kate Moss. In the first decade of the twenty-first century, the sensual body image of Britney Spears, Christina Aguilera, and Jennifer Lopez has captured the attention of media and minors alike. Images such as these bombard each of us daily. Although the body trends may change, the message is clear: thin is in and beauty is everything.

People magazine polled one thousand women about their bodies and how the images of Hollywood's stars influence their self-esteem. Only one in ten said they were completely satisfied with their bodies. Eighty percent said images of women on TV and in movies, fashion magazines, and advertising made them feel insecure about their looks. Sixty percent were not satisfied with their weight. Thirty-four percent would consider plastic surgery.[1]

According to Lindy Beam, clinical psychologist and *Reviving Ophelia* author Mary Pipher reports, "Research shows that virtually all women are ashamed of their bodies. It used to be adult women [and] teenage girls who were ashamed, but now you see the shame down to very young girls—10, 11 years old. Society's standard of beauty is an image that is literally just short of starvation for most women."[2]

"Many girls are feeling pressured to be the impossible—The Perfect Girl."

Writing in *Girls' Life* magazine, Roni Cohen-Sandler reveals that girls today "feel like they have to be all-around superstars. Not just really strong at one thing…but pretty stellar at almost everything. In other words, many girls are feeling pressured to be the impossible—The Perfect Girl. More and more girls are giving themselves impossible goals and falling short of what they think is ideal."[3]

Feelings of insecurity are masked behind "Girl Power" and a strong feminist mindset. Teen and women's magazines reinforce the self-actualization message by emphasizing empowerment and self-reliance, which can fuel the pressure to be "in charge" and "have it all together."

What image are you pursuing? What is your definition of the perfect girl, the feminine ideal? And where has your search taken you?

Join me on a journey. I'll describe my personal struggle with an eating disorder, and other problems, as I found myself pursuing the "ideal image." We'll explore the heart issues that fueled my elusive quest. Then I'll share the discoveries I've made that have given me hope and helped me to live life with an open, healed heart.

If you identify with some of the core issues we'll discuss, I pray you will be able to find the freedom to experience life to the fullest. Ideal or not, we can embrace life as a journey toward the freedom of discovering our true identity and worth. Let's get started!

CHAPTER 1

PURSUiNG
the iDEAL

D on't you enjoy a good love story, especially when Prince Charming comes to rescue the princess and whisk her away to his castle? We imagine ourselves as either the heroine or the sought after maiden—beautiful, exotic, charming. It's part of our human nature to desire romance, adventure, and passion. We want life to be like those fairy tales with exciting plots and happy endings. We dream, "If only this will happen, then everything will be perfect and I will be happy." We even try to create our own ideal story.

An ideal is a standard of perfection, beauty, or excellence, or a person who exemplifies our ideal, often taken as a model for imitation. But in reality, the ideal exists only in our mind. It's imaginary. This character isn't real, and like playing a part in a drama, we have to act out the part, sometimes even putting on a mask. I was in drama club in high school and played some funny parts: a millionaire named Alonzo B. Goldmine (I went to an all-girls school), an island girl in *South Pacific*, and a lady-in-waiting in *The Princess and the Pea*. One time I played a dancing flower in *Wizard of Oz*. As I danced across the stage, looking so perfect, I suddenly messed up. I forgot my dance steps and was completely embarrassed. My petals wilted. The endless search for "ideal" can hinder the real role for which we were created.

Several events in junior high school triggered my desire for the ideal body. The most memorable was at the swimming pool one summer. I wore a red-and-white polka-dot bikini and was flattered by the attention I received from boys. I realized then that having the right body brought attention and boyfriends. I remember thinking, *I don't ever want to get fat.* Thus began my endless creative dieting plans. I've always been extremely social, so my increasing popularity with boys fed my craving for the model body.

> My increasing popularity with boys fed my craving for the model body.

My quest for the ideal continued in high school. I desperately wanted to be a cheerleader. I grew up in a very social, sports-oriented family with four very athletic brothers and one younger sister. My father had been a star athlete in high school, so there was a tremendous incentive for all of us to succeed in athletics. As an incoming freshman, I idealized Mickey, the cheerleading captain who had a fine boyfriend. To make the cheerleading squad would be the ultimate! I practiced splits, jumps, and flips until I was dizzy. With one open spot on the squad, I knew it was going to be tough to make it. But after all that work, can you believe my best friend made it and not me? I was devastated.

True to form, I tried to hide my deep disappointment and kept practicing for the next year. Perseverance paid off. My sophomore year, I made the squad. I had achieved my goal—I had arrived! I thrived on the attention, recognition, and the fun camaraderie of the squad. But too soon I found out how fragile my image could be. At one game, I was particularly excited because a guy I wanted to impress was in the stands. Focusing more on him than on my backwards summersault, I landed in my split position on top of my partner. Because I was supposed to have landed in front of her, the situation was completely embarrassing. I laughed hysterically and lost control of my bladder, leaving a puddle on the gym floor, not to mention my uniform. So much for the stellar impression I was trying to make! Maybe this should have been a clue as to how disastrous this pursuit of the ideal could become. My quest for perfection was destined to fail.

I was off to the next challenge in my pursuit of the "ideal life": I set my sights on tall, dark, and handsome Tom. He was a buff wrestler and a star football player who later played pro-ball. Not only was he athletic and good-looking, but he was also very nice. Although I went to an all-girls' school, I had the opportunity to invite him to a dance. I worked up my nerve to ask him after circling around Steak 'n Shake, where everybody was hanging out. He actually said yes! We hit it off, and he invited me to his prom.

My dad was just as impressed with Tom as I was. In fact, he took more pictures before the dance than I can ever remember him taking in my life. I was a little embarrassed, but proud at the same time. Life was sweet, and I was totally infatuated with Tom. But then, other girls began inviting him to dances, and suddenly there went my dream boyfriend. Now that he was in demand, there was no time left for me. My heart was crushed. I didn't know what to do with my sadness and disappointment, so I buried those feelings deep inside and moved on as I looked for another "ideal guy."

My pursuit went beyond love and acceptance. Significance and performance were extremely important to me as well. I strove for good grades to please my parents and myself. My involvement in student council put me in a leadership position, which I loved. Drama and pep clubs fed into my craving for an audience. Because I thrived on popularity, I wanted to be friends with everybody, not just with one group. I cared about all the girls at my school, and friends came to me seeking counsel and help. It was wonderful to be able to help them. I was even voted the "Friendliest Girl" two years at my high school.

Appearances Are Deceiving

On the outside, everything looked picture perfect, as if I had no wants. I was confident when things went well, but deep inside I felt insecure whenever I encountered an emotion that wasn't "positive." Ever felt that way? Being "up" was what was expected of me; anything else was unacceptable. I repeatedly set my sights on something else to attain, another adventure to have, or a mountain to climb. It was natural for me to try to create what I envisioned as an ideal life, but trying to keep up that image became a driving force.

It was great fun growing up in a family of six children: my wild older brother, Jack, then me, Danny, Karen, Keith, and Mark —all about eighteen months apart in age. Our home seemed to be the center of activity for the whole neighborhood. During my high school years, Jack was definitely a challenge for my mom and dad, always full of surprises. Several times the police showed up at our door, asking for "Crash Wilson" (as we called Jack) who had wrecked another car.

Sometimes Jack and Dad got into big arguments, and I often found myself trying to make peace between them. I couldn't stand it when they would yell at each other. Anger and fighting upset my "ideal" world, so I did everything I could to solve these problems, eagerly taking on the role of peacemaker.

I didn't want to rock the boat since there was enough stress in our home with Jack's experiences. He would often show up at dances where I was, and I can remember dreading seeing him and his gang arrive. I had a love-hate relationship with his friends. I cared about them, yet I hated that they thrived on starting fights, or "rumbles," at the worst possible times.

Can you believe that at a homecoming dance, my brother and his gang showed up, jumped onto the stage, and literally dethroned the king? They threw him off the stage and started a big fight. Talk about humiliating! No mischievous activity of mine would even compare with Jack's antics, so I was considered a "good girl." Following my tendency to be performance-oriented, I pictured what my parents would expect of me, and I was determined to be that perfect daughter for them.

Because I came from a strong religious background, I also thought God expected certain behaviors and standards from me. I therefore put enormous pressure on myself to perform for God, as well as other people. I really loved God, as best I knew how. As a little girl I had a special desire to know Him and felt He had a purpose for my life. As long as I lived "according to the rules," I felt accepted by God. There was an uneasiness, though, as I faced feelings and emotions that seemed unacceptable or less than perfect. Although I prided myself on being a "good person," the standard always seemed to be just beyond my reach.

Eating Disorder Disorders My Life

Because I put pressure on myself to look and act a certain way, life was good if I met my self-imposed standards, but any "failure" led to anxiety. One of the key gauges of my ideal was my weight. Unfortunately, after each cheerleading practice, our squad would indulge in pizzas and snacks. Until this time, I was in great shape, but all the snacking took its toll. Despite the workouts, I began to get a little chunky.

To lose the extra pounds, I experimented with fad diets and became almost obsessed with losing weight. This was not uncommon. It seemed like every girl in high school was on a diet. One day around the lunch table, a girlfriend innocently announced, "I've discovered this great way to lose weight!" She certainly captured our attention; we all wanted to know what it was. She explained, "You just stick your finger down your throat and make yourself sick." We all thought that was totally gross and insane and couldn't believe anyone would actually do that.

Not long after that is when I came home from the dance feeling rejected that the guy I cared for wasn't interested in me. Depressed about eating so much and fearful of gaining weight, I remembered my girlfriend's new "diet plan."

I tried it. It was hard at first, trying to make myself gag, but I eventually managed to throw up. It was a temporary relief to rid myself of all the excess calories, but it was a horrible experience. I promised myself that I would never do it again. The only problem was, I became hooked on a simple solution to the complex problem of learning to deal with life's ups and downs. Though bingeing and purging, what I now know is called bulimia, started out as a one-time experience, it gradually took over my life. I vividly remember preparing cake mixes, pancake mixes, or cookie dough and eating the whole bowl of batter. And the night I ate a whole peach pie, I rode my bike furiously to the store to buy another before my mother could miss the first one. I was also trying to exercise away the additional calories. I'm amazed that I could have hidden these activities from my family.

What often triggered my overeating was some disappointment or emotion that I couldn't control. I always appeared happy, but I didn't know how to deal with negative emotions. In my mind, negative feelings like sadness, worry, anger, and depression were unacceptable. I hadn't learned how to recognize my feelings as normal, as a gift from God to help me know that an area in my life needs my attention. No one knew that inward side of me—not even me. I could counsel all my friends, but I could not counsel myself. Instead, I suppressed my feelings, using food as my coping mechanism.

What started out as a simple diet trick when I was a high school junior ended up being addictive for me and, eventually, destructive. As I look back, I see now that I was striving for the perfect body, for acceptance from boyfriends, and for a way to please my parents and God. I was a slave to the "ideal" world I'd created!

I didn't know what was wrong with me, but I soon realized that I could not control this new "diet technique." I was either starving myself or gorging myself and then making myself sick. I knew my habits were neither right nor healthy. After each ritual, I would feel a brief sense of relief, but then the guilt would overwhelm me. One night I tried to talk to my mother about this problem, but I didn't make my struggle clear enough. She just didn't get it! She dismissed my concern and guilt by telling me not to worry about it, that everyone has trouble with their weight from time to time. I was sinking further and further into this trap, and didn't see any way of escape.

My mother was such a positive person. If she couldn't help me, who could? Because my mask had become a part of my personality, even my mom couldn't see through it. She didn't have a clue that I was struggling so seriously. Besides, Mom had her hands full with Jack's antics and the needs of four other children. As the second oldest in a large family, I took on the responsibility of meeting the others' needs and being a peacemaker. My own problems and needs seemed selfish to me, which became another reason to bury them like my feelings and ignore them.

After I graduated, I was excited about going away to college so I could get over this problem and make a new start. But as I entered college, the bulimia only escalated. The pressure to perform in every area seemed to intensify in college, and food had become my sole way of coping. Living in the dorm gave me the perfect opportunity to overeat in the cafeteria, then get rid of it all in private. After joining a sorority, I found myself sneaking into the kitchen and stealing food to satisfy my starving soul. My thoughts constantly revolved around food: What should I eat? What should I not eat? When would I get rid of what I did eat? I was 5'2" and dropped from 130 pounds at my heaviest in high school to a mere 96 pounds in college. At my lowest weight I looked extremely thin, yet I still considered my stomach to be fat.

I knew that I was hurting my body, but it didn't matter to me; I was hooked.

The secretive cycle of bingeing and purging became increasingly easy, but it was destroying my health. My eyes were puffy and my raw throat bled from the purging. Sometimes I did this several times a day. No one—not my parents, not my high school or college friends—knew what I was doing for a long time. I knew that I was hurting my body, but it didn't matter to me; I was hooked. Over and over I'd vow never to do it again, starving myself for a while and then failing again as I binged and purged.

As my bulimia continued to worsen, people finally began to notice that I was getting skinnier. Of course, I was determined to maintain my thin figure; it was part of my ideal image. During my freshman year of college, I pledged a great party sorority and dated the president of a fraternity. One night at a fraternity "mini-skirt" party, I won a six-pack of beer for wearing the shortest mini-skirt. I even made extra money by modeling a bikini in a storefront window, supposedly to advertise Maytag washing machines. Being thin definitely had its advantages. I felt attractive and in control.

However, at the time I not only struggled with an eating disorder, I was compromising my moral convictions. I was in a sorority that required its members to attend three fraternity keggers each week! I began to drink too much, which led me to let down my guard and get involved physically with guys in ways that I never would have before. This just added to my shame and brought all the confusion in my life to a boiling point. Something had to change!

By this time, I had accumulated loads of demerits for missing my dorm curfew. In fact, I held the record for the most demerits of all the freshmen girls. What an honor that was!

One night I arrived late, and drunk—and with a drunken date! Was I in big trouble! What began as social drinking had gotten out of hand. Drinking became another way to keep up the image. The same inner turmoil that led to my compulsive overeating also led to my compulsive drinking. The next morning I attended church with a hangover. Though barely able to think, I recognized the irony of my situation. It's as if God were asking me, "Nancy, is this what you really want your life to be like? You're barely coherent, and you're trying to perform for Me here at church, but you really don't know Me."

I felt like I had failed God, and that made me very sad.

My pursuit of the ideal had not brought me closer to perfect, but further from it. I had reached a crisis point. But I was about to discover the Source of a truly ideal life.

CHAPTER 2

FiNDiNG the TRUTH

I felt like I was caught in a trap. Feeling helpless and hopeless that I would ever get better, I slid into deep depression. I remember crying out to God, "Oh God, if you're real, please help me!"

Having been brought up in church, I thought I knew God. But somehow it didn't seem that God was helping me. I had tried to overcome my eating disorder through my own efforts—fasting after I binged and purged, making promises to myself and God, and using my own will power—to no avail. I was desperate. I had come to the end of myself. I would cry myself to sleep at night, praying, "God, please show me what is wrong with me and how I can change."

Then something life-changing happened. One night as I returned from a party, disillusioned with yet another relationship, I was invited to a popcorn party on my dorm floor. The party theme was relationships. The friends who invited me had no idea what was going on inside of me. They just cared about me and sensed I was searching. The timing was perfect, since I was looking for real answers to my very real issues.

As relationships were discussed, my curiosity was piqued when one of the women, Marcie, shared that God wanted us to have a personal relationship with Him. She described God's unconditional love and His care for us. For the first time, my eyes were opened to a new kind of love, a new level of acceptance, and a freedom from performing. One of my girlfriends in my dorm told how she had come to know God in a very personal and intimate way. Marcie explained further that I didn't need to measure up to any standard, because God didn't expect me to be perfect or "have it all together" before He would accept me. Since He had uniquely created me and had a purpose for my life, He loved me the way I was.

> My eyes were opened to a new kind of love, and a freedom from performing.

At that party I learned that God had made me for Himself. In all my pursuits for the ideal, I was simply searching for Him. I began to understand that I had been striving to overcome feelings of inadequacy and imperfection, and trying to control my life in order to fit into my standard of perfection. This was all a result of a separation between a very imperfect me and a very perfect God, a gap that I could never bridge on my own.

How tragic if this separation were the final destination of my life. That night I learned that God, my heavenly Father, loved me so much that He wanted me to know of His unconditional love and acceptance. So He sent His Son, Jesus, to die on the cross in my place, to pay the debt for all of my sins, which I could never pay on my own. This grace—this unmerited favor —is an incredible gift from God, something I could never earn.

What a revelation this was to me! Was it too good to be true? How could God love me in my unworthy state? I was well aware of my sins, failings, shortcomings, compromises, confusion, selfishness, and bondage. But Jesus laid down His own life as a perfect sacrifice in order to provide my forgiveness so I could have a relationship with God. And there is no greater love than someone laying down his life for another. I finally understood what the good news of the gospel really is: it's a love story born in the heart of a passionate God desiring a love relationship with each one of us individually.

Through Jesus, God extends to each of us an invitation to become His child: "To all who received him, to those who believed in his name, he gave the right to become children of God—children born not of natural descent, nor of human decision or a husband's will, but born of God" (John 1:12,13). Salvation is not what I can do for God, but recognizing my need for Him, responding to His amazing love, and trusting Jesus as my personal Savior and Lord.

Though I had known about Jesus, I had never personally responded to His offer of forgiveness. No one could make that choice for me; His love required a personal response. It was one I joyfully made as tears streamed down my cheeks. It was as if God had brought me to the place where I wanted real answers, then He met me in that place. He truly had heard my cries for help! These truths were new to me and I did not understand them immediately. But I understood enough to know that I wanted to ask Jesus to forgive me, to come live in my life, to heal my heart, and to enable me to have a relationship with my heavenly Father.

So I prayed a simple, life-changing prayer asking God for forgiveness and giving my life, though full of weakness and sin, to Jesus. This was the beginning of my personal relationship with Jesus, the beginning of experiencing His love and understanding my new identity as a beloved daughter of my heavenly Father. Only He could set me free from my sins, including my eating disorder.

Although finally free and given a new life, I still needed God's help to replace my old thought patterns. So complete freedom from the eating disorder, and from the bondage of striving for perfection and approval, would take time. My old thought patterns about myself involved a case of "mistaken identity"; I thought I was a failure because I didn't measure up to my standards. I realized that I had been basing my identity and self-worth on the wrong measuring system: the media's images of beauty and the world's false definitions of success and significance. Over time, I learned to measure my worth accurately according to God's value system: He valued me as a person, both inside and out, regardless of my appearance or performance.

By having me face the reality of my life, God helped me deal with wrong thought patterns about myself and my pursuit of the ideal. My new life in Christ freed me to delve deeper within and to take a critical look at what was true in my life.

The Awful Truth

There I was one evening, partying at the Sig Ep house, talking about my newfound faith; hours later, I was in my sorority bathroom, hunched over the toilet, purposely gagging myself. What in the world would drive me to this compulsive behavior? This toxic act had become a life-and-death matter, and a problem that went much deeper than food. It was an issue at the very core of my heart. A Band-Aid solution would not work; major surgery was required.

These were times of great despair. Addicted to a harmful way of coping with my feelings, I could not measure up to my own standards for my body, performance, or acceptance. But what deep need drove me to this point? How did I get to this place?

Apart from God's help throughout this journey, I don't believe I could have figured out some of the complex needs that I was trying to meet.

The Radical Truth

In John chapter 4, the Bible shares a great story of Jesus encountering a woman in Samaria. In the days of Jesus' earthly life, it was uncommon for men to interact with women in public, and nearly unheard of for men to *initiate* a public conversation with women. In addition, the Jews and Samaritans intensely disliked each other.

As the apostle John tells us, Jesus approached this woman at a well and asked her, "Will you give me a drink?" Because of the social norms, she was amazed that Jesus had made such a request of her, a Samaritan woman. She responded, "You are a Jew and I am a Samaritan woman. How can you ask me for a drink?" But Jesus said, "If you knew the gift of God and who it is that is asking you for a drink, you would have asked him and he would have given you living water."

Although Jesus initially asked for a physical drink, He really intended to discuss a spiritual thirst-quencher. What began as a conversation to meet a physical need quickly led to a discussion about meeting the Samaritan woman's deepest needs.

Jesus knew the woman was unsuccessfully trying to quench her spiritual thirst with physical water. He told her, "Everyone who drinks this water will be thirsty again. But whoever drinks the water I give him will never thirst. Indeed, the water I give him will become in him a spring of water welling up to eternal life." Intrigued by His comments, the woman naturally wanted this water. She said, "Sir, give me this water so that I won't get thirsty and have to keep coming here to draw water."

Truly, the woman's response is typical of us all. We want whatever it is that will satisfy our thirst. But until we actually find the source, we go from well to well, trying different potions. In my pursuit of the ideal, I drank from the many empty wells I have just shared with you. Each well may represent a different thirst—a deep desire for love and acceptance, the pursuit of an ideal image or appearance, or significance and purpose in life.

The well of popularity may offer approval that quenches our thirst temporarily, but when we experience rejection or hurt, we are again thirsty and our empty heart longs for something else to fill it. We may then look to the well of significance and accomplishments, thinking that if we can satisfy our need for worth, we will be fulfilled . . . only to find ourselves disappointed when we don't measure up or reach our potential. Drinking from empty wells can open our hearts to lots of pain and disillusionment.

But Jesus saw beneath the surface and addressed the deepest need of the Samaritan woman's heart, the longing for value and worth. When He tapped into her real need, He revealed His knowledge that she had five husbands and that the man she was living with was not her husband. Jesus spoke the truth, and the woman was shocked that He knew everything about her. Perhaps what won her heart was that she experienced Jesus' love and acceptance even though He knew the complete depth of her sin and need.

How could she resist such grace and truth demonstrated through Jesus' acceptance of her? The woman immediately left her water jar and ran back to her town to tell the people, "Come, see a man who told me everything I ever did. Could this be the Christ?" And because of her experience, many from the town came to meet Jesus.

Before her encounter with Jesus, the Samaritan woman's reality was to go from man to man, searching for the ideal in relationships that left her empty. She came to realize that her ideal without God was merely a counterfeit. She exchanged her water jar for the "real deal" about life.

The "real deal" is that we live in a world that cannot give us what we need. The One who created us and loves us just the way we are is the only One who can satisfy the deepest needs of our soul. To love and be loved for who we are, apart from our appearance or performance, is a core need of every human being. For this to happen, we must each pull down the barrier around our heart. We must remove the ribbon wrapped around our soul's exterior, and open up and look at what is inside. This leads to our becoming authentic with God. He can handle it! In fact, this is the very reason Jesus came to earth. Our loving Father sent Him to bear our pain and loss caused by the disastrous effects of sin. Whether we deliberately chose to go down our own destructive path, or were the victim of another's sin and evil choices, He can heal us, giving us renewed hope to face the future. In the beautiful Book of Isaiah, the prophet foretells the coming of our Savior and describes His destiny and purpose. Ponder these amazing truths:

> Who believes what we've heard and seen? Who would have thought God's saving power would look like this? The servant grew up before God—a scrawny seedling, a scrubby plant in a parched field. There was nothing attractive about him, nothing to cause us to take a second look. He was looked down on and passed over, a man who suffered, who knew pain firsthand. One look at him and people turned away. We looked down on him, thought he was scum. But the fact is, it was *our* pains he carried—*our* disfigurements, all the things wrong with *us*. We thought he brought it on himself, that God was punishing him for his own failures. But it was *our* sins that did that to him, that ripped and tore and crushed him—*our sins!*
>
> He took the punishment, and that made us whole.

Through his bruises we get healed. We're all like sheep who've wandered off and gotten lost. We've all done our own thing, gone our own way. And God has piled all our sins, everything we've done wrong, on him, on him. (Isaiah 53:1–6, *The Message*, emphasis added)

This is radical truth! He was not known by His image, but by His sacrificial love. The God who created the universe and formed each of us as His precious creation came personally to rescue us from our sin and shame. Nothing is too shocking or too shameful for His suffering on the cross to cover and heal. That is exactly why He came: to die for you and for me, and for a world desperate for healing from the ravages of sin.

The cross crosses out all of our sin. My healing has come as I have embraced what Jesus Christ has done for me on the cross.

This healing has been a process, one through which I am still going. The overt symptoms of my eating disorder are past, but I still must deal with the heart issues. Understanding and accepting my needs, desires, fears, and limitations has been a growth experience.

It takes courage to identify the unhealthy motivations that propel me. Unchecked, these issues could once again drive me to compulsive behavior or a destructive lifestyle. This can also involve an unhealthy introspection of myself and my actions, a preoccupation with how I am doing or how people are perceiving me. My thoughts could be centered on the illusive "if onlys": if only I could accomplish this; if only I could achieve that; if only I could have that perfect man to love me. But the reality is that these are just Band-Aids we seek to cover our wounds.

For true healing to take place, we must face the fact that we are wounded. In my case, this meant finding the courage to look at my childhood and understand what caused some of my deepest needs. I had to acknowledge my fear of not being loved, accepted, valuable, or worthwhile—all based on my not measuring up to an "ideal image" or not fulfilling standards set by myself or others.

Coming to terms with my value, completely unrelated to any external source, was so significant and freeing. You see, perfect love casts out all fear. Because God's love is perfect and complete, we don't have to be afraid. He heals our spirits and restores us. We can't hide our wounds and weaknesses, but rather we must face them and learn to overcome them. We do this by applying the healing ointment of truth, which is God's amazing, incredible, overwhelming, unconditional love and forgiveness.

Recently, I was at a special place in Phoenix, Arizona, called Canaan in the Desert, where I love to go whenever I can to rest, reflect, and write. It has a prayer garden, a little taste of heaven on earth, where my heart is filled with fresh reminders of Jesus' love and sacrifice for me.

My healing has come as I have embraced what Jesus has done for me on the cross.

Early one morning as the sun was rising, I hiked up a nearby mountain. I embarked on my journey after stopping to drink from the Fountain of the Father's Goodness—a beautiful fountain on the grounds which is continually flowing with refreshing water. There in the midst of the peaceful prayer garden, with little rabbits playing and birds joyfully singing, sits this fountain engraved with the words: "Father of GOODNESS, Father of LOVE, Father of FAITHFULNESS, Father of MERCY, Father of GRACE, Father of PATIENCE." Each quality of God has a drinking spout. On this morning, I eagerly drank from the "Father of Patience" spout as I remembered how kind and patient my heavenly Father had been since I began my journey with Him many years ago. This refreshing truth will sustain you as you face the realities of your life. My Father God reminded me as I hiked the rugged mountain, "I will be with you, strengthening you and guiding you, on each mountain I call you to climb."

As I gazed at the majestic view from the top, I was awestruck with the new perspective I was given. Yes indeed, our Father of love, faithfulness, goodness, grace, mercy, and patience will take us by the hand as He directs our journey onward.

So be courageous; let's hike up yet another mountain on this journey, the journey of facing what is real.

The Pursuit
Seeking to fill my heart
Began an innocent start;

Longing for needs to be filled
Only temporarily thrilled;

Chasing after my ideal,
Avoiding facing the real;

Falling into the snare
Quickly led to despair;

Crying, "God, are you there?"
Was my desperate prayer;

Amazing love rescued me,
Paid the price to set me free;

Gazing at Calvary's cross,
Where Jesus bore my sin and loss;

Pursuing me as His own,
My Father's love is shown;

Capturing my devotion,
Healing my emotion;

Finding the Truth

Liberating truth is mine,
Freeing me to shine;

Declaring to everyone,
"Come to the Son!"

Preparing as an eager bride,
To forever reign at His side.

CHAPTER 3

FACiNG WHAT iS REAL

I grew up playing with Barbie, Ken, and Skipper—and all the accessories: the car, the house, and the clothes. Since my childhood, Barbie has come a long way. She's now in her forties, looking as good as ever, and is the most versatile professional woman I've ever known. She comes in nearly every nationality and her influence is worldwide. Amazingly, Barbie has always had a boyfriend and siblings, but never parents, a husband, or children.

Yet we need to remember, Barbie is *not* real. Did you know that Barbie's real-life measurements would be 40-18-32? And at a life-size height of 5'7" and weighing 100 pounds, if she didn't topple over, she'd at the very least have intense back pain all her life.[1]

As a young girl, playing with Barbie offered countless opportunities to imagine the ideal: the ideal body, the ideal boyfriend, the ideal life. What I didn't realize is that my childhood imaginations grew into teenage goals.

Researchers at the University of Arizona suspected there was a connection between little girls playing with Barbie and bigger girls thinking they have to look like Barbie. The study found that 90 percent of the Caucasian teenagers surveyed expressed dissatisfaction with their bodies, and many saw dieting as a panacea. And they were united in their description of the perfect girl: 5'7" tall, weighing just over 100 pounds, with long legs and flowing hair. Based on the teens' responses, the researchers concluded that the ideal girl was essentially a living Barbie doll. [2]

New York Times columnist Anna Quindlen cited a study where 83 percent of the girls surveyed wanted to lose weight, even though 62 percent were in the normal weight range.[3] She described teen girls as having a distorted fun-house image of their own bodies. And we all know a fun-house mirror does not give us a realistic picture of ourselves.

> The researchers concluded that the ideal girl was essentially a living Barbie doll.

Dissatisfaction with their physical traits is an almost universal theme for American women. Perhaps you don't like your weight, your height, your hair, your complexion, your figure, or your nose. You're not alone. Women find numerous approaches to fixing these "problems," including the growing popularity of plastic surgery among young women. Not only do we not like the way we look, we don't like who we are. We're driven to prove that we are somebody since "image is everything"! Even successful women feel the same way. Listen to what one famous woman had to say:

> I have an iron will, and all of my will had always been to conquer some horrible feeling of inadequacy. I'm always struggling with that fear. I push past one spell of it and I

discover myself as a special human being, and then I get to another stage and think I'm mediocre, and I'm uninteresting. And I find a way to get myself out of that again and again. My drive in life is from this horrible feeling of mediocrity. That's always been pushing me, pushing me. Because even though I've become somebody, I still have to prove that I'm SOMEBODY. My struggle has never ended, and it probably never will.[4]

That quote, surprisingly, is from Madonna, "the Material Girl." She feels compelled to continually try to prove that she's somebody, even though in the world's eyes she already is somebody. To read between the lines, Madonna is acknowledging that worldly success doesn't satisfy our souls. Friend, that is reality!

Another pop icon seems to have the same self-doubt. In an article about Britney Spears entitled "Britney's new show doesn't solve her identity crisis," the writer tells us:

At nearly 20, the world's most famous ex-Mouseketeer ... still doesn't seem to know who she is. Previous teen stars as diverse as Debbie Gibson and Fiona Apple have carved out personal and musical identities that, love 'em and hate 'em, were distinctive and genuine. Spears, in contrast, continues to come across as a highly polished cipher ... Addressing her critics at one point, Spears rightfully noted, "I'm not a little girl anymore." But as a performer, she still seems like a kid playing dress-up with some very expensive clothes.[5]

Even the rich and famous struggle to know who they are and what is real in their lives. It is easy to see the breakdown between image and true satisfaction in the lives of popular actresses, teen idols, even princesses. Though it may seem glamorous to be on a magazine cover or in the media, we hear so many stories of painful lives behind the scenes.

Princess Diana and Sarah Ferguson, the Dutchess of York, have both shared struggles with eating disorders. Recently, Sarah Ferguson has written about her struggle and shared openly on television.

> Now 41 years old, [Sarah Ferguson's] weight has yo-yoed since she was 12, when her mother left her father to marry another man and move to Argentina.
>
> "I've been an emotional eater since I was a teenager," she would later tell me. With her mother gone, Ferguson comforted herself with fattening foods they had enjoyed together—sausages, egg salad, pate. "I overate to compensate for my feelings. I didn't want to express to my mother that I was angry or sad that she'd left me." Soon after, she began the fad-diet shuffle, shedding pounds rapidly only to regain them when her emotions pointed her toward food.[6]

I can relate with Sarah's reliance upon food as a comfort to deal with emotional stresses. Many of us can. But how do these patterns of behavior get established?

As we've seen, the ideals we strive for, and the images we portray, are very often not what's real. Now we are going to examine a key element in facing reality—our family.

Facing Your Family Background

The role our parents play in our lives is amazingly significant. The pressure for perfection is sometimes attributed to fathers who have been emotionally distant or preoccupied with their careers, or to an overly controlling mother who is perfectionistic and demanding.

Whatever imperfections are found in your family, you are not alone. There is no perfect family. All parents are less than ideal, trying to cope with life in the way they have learned. However, you are not stuck as a victim, but through God's help can unravel some unhealthy patterns and establish new ones.

Let's look at a case study. Sondra's troubles began in her early teen years. At age 14, she was interested in boys, but they didn't seem to return her interest. Maybe ten pounds overweight, she thought the extra pounds were a turnoff to boys. Her mother encouraged her to lose weight, frequently giving her articles on the latest diet fads. Meticulous about appearance, Sondra's father was subtly critical of her looks and often made comments about her clothes, hair, and weight. Her younger brother teased her, calling her "Porky." Even Sondra's gymnastics instructor told her she could make the school team if she dropped a few pounds.

Determined to lose weight, Sondra ate fewer and fewer calories and exercised more and more. Once she had lost some weight, her parents noticed, her brother stopped calling her names, the guys whistled at her, and she made the gymnastics team.

But now she was hooked. What began as a diet developed into a condition called anorexia nervosa. Her weight continued dropping, first to 100 pounds, then to 90. Her parents, who loved her very much, were alarmed. They warned her not to take dieting so seriously. They even bribed her with a new wardrobe if she gained a little weight.

Already, Sondra had become consumed with the belief that by looking right she would gain her parents' acceptance. More than anything, she wanted to measure up to their expectations, as she perceived them.

Eventually, Sondra found help for her anorexia. But then she began craving all the foods that for years she had denied herself while dieting. What resulted was the binge-purge cycle of bulimia, which she struggled with for several years. Tragically, at age 33, Sondra died from a heart attack due to the strain her eating disorders had placed on her organs.[7] This story ends without a happy ending; however, it doesn't have to be that way.

During my college years, I struggled desperately to understand my own tendency to succumb to an eating disorder. Upon later reflection I realized that while growing up, I had a tremendous desire to please my parents, especially my dad. Like most girls, I longed for my father's approval, though at the time I didn't realize the effect this longing would have on me.

Dad was an accomplished businessman and a great athlete. He was not only hardworking, athletic, successful, and funny, but also a very driven man. He had overcome many challenges to establish his own business. Since he was supporting six children in private school, his work schedule was incredibly demanding. Understandably, he wasn't always available to give me the kind of emotional support that I sought.

Because I admired and loved my dad so much, his approval had the power to shape my self-esteem. Never doubting he loved me, I secretly longed for more affirmation from him and more time together. Perhaps I subconsciously felt that if I could perform well and accomplish things, he would be pleased with me and would love me more. As part of a big family, I took on the role of the responsible, older daughter. I succeeded in playing the part, but this served to develop a mindset in which my worth was based on my performance.

One day as we were preparing to leave a father/daughter banquet, I remember my dad saying to me, "Looks like you're gaining some weight." He said it in passing and didn't mean much by the offhand remark, yet his words affected me deeply. I began thinking how much I was not measuring up since I had added pounds. I worried, *What am I going to do? I've got to lose this weight.*

That was one of the trigger points for my overemphasis on having the ideal body. In later years, Dad and I talked about this. He had no idea how deeply his approval affected me. I don't think most fathers really understand this innate desire in every little girl to win her daddy's heart. Some of us spend much of our energy trying to gain our father's attention, approval, and affection. Truthfully, many of us have been hurt because our earthly fathers are imperfect and often fall short of meeting our emotional needs. And in some families, the father is absent, distant, or even abusive. You may have deep wounds caused by your father or his lack of demonstrated love. Your pain is real, but healing is available.

You need to look honestly at your family situation. Remember, no family is perfect. If your family situation is less than ideal, know that God sees and cares about you. He can fill any needs in your life because He is a perfect Father. He loves you and wants to affirm you. But until you look at some of the hurts in your family and face any wounds there, you won't be able to move forward and experience your healing.

It doesn't matter what stage of life you find yourself in, it's never too late to revisit the foundation of your belief system about yourself. I recently talked with the husband of a woman who had been abused emotionally and physically as a child. He shared his desire to help her get beyond her past and develop her confidence in who God made her to be. He is very handsome, and she always feels inferior and insecure around other women. Unless she deals with the lies that have affected her identity, she will always grapple with these feelings of inadequacy.

As I've traveled around the world ministering to women of all ages, I find that the need is the same. We all have a deep need to be known, loved, and cherished. In Africa, I have seen the hunger for a father's love, since so many have lost parents to AIDS. In Slovakia and other Eastern European countries, alcoholism is very prevalent, often leading to abuse in the home. In the Middle East, women struggle with a sense of worth due to severe mistreatment and lack of equal rights in some places. In

America, and around the world, the effects of pornography and sexual perversion have led to devastating cases of fathers sexually abusing their daughters. My heart breaks as I think of those who have been the victims of these traumatic acts.

These cases are severe, but whether you have been deeply wounded or just disappointed in your relationship with your family, it can affect your sense of self-worth. Jennifer is a 13-year-old friend of mine whose mother is suffering the consequences of a very painful childhood. Due to her emotional abuse as a young girl, she battles depression and physical problems, which are now having an effect on Jennifer.

> Whatever our family situation has been, we don't have to repeat the unhealthy pattern.

Jennifer wants to break out and be her own person but feels stuck as she faces her mother's desire to control her and her dad's super-strict rules. To establish her own identity, she began wearing black, alternative-style clothes, and her parents don't like it. In another effort to control her life, Jennifer started cutting her wrists with a razor. When I took her out to talk, she confided that she had a very low self-image and felt worthless.

Jennifer and I talked truthfully about her family dynamics and how she can deal with them in a healthy way. It will take a process of being honest with her parents and herself. She and her parents have a ways to go, but are on the path to healing.

No matter what our family situation has been, we don't have to repeat the unhealthy pattern. We can learn to evaluate the pros and cons of our parents' actions, recognizing all the positive things they modeled, as well as dealing with the negative. God can give you the strength to be different. He may want to use you to break a cycle of sin that has been passed from generation to generation.

As we continue our journey, we will take a look at our beliefs about ourselves to see where we may have believed a lie instead of God's truth.

Facing the Lies

In addition to considering our unique family backgrounds, it is crucial to identify any lies we have come to believe about ourselves. In this task, I've been greatly helped by several resources. Dr. Neil Anderson has some excellent books that God used to teach me about my new identity in Christ. As I grew in understanding of how God sees me, I was then able to discover more clearly my wrong belief patterns. Dawson McAllister and Robert S. McGee have discussed these lies about our self-worth extensively in their workbook, *Search for Significance*.[8] Let's briefly look at these valuable insights.

Lie 1: *We have to perform in order to feel good about ourselves.* I felt I had to achieve something in order to be of value. Being involved in student council, cheerleading, getting good grades, being popular—these achievements made me feel worthy, or so I thought. The problem was there was always one more thing to achieve. My quest was elusive; I was never content, but was continually restless for the next accomplishment.

Where do you find your worth? Perhaps you find it in making good grades, dating a special person, excelling in music or athletics, earning a lot of money, or owning a business. Though all these may be worthy goals, they don't define our value.

This performance treadmill can drive us to constantly need to achieve more to keep up an image. Consider the experience of Olympic gymnast Nancy Thies Marshall:

> The attention I received from the Olympics went a long way to fulfill my teenage longing for acceptance. I loved

feeling famous. I started believing that in order to be accepted I had to make Olympic teams in everything I did. I had to keep up my image. I had a hard time liking myself when I wasn't outstanding, which was most of the time.[9]

If we buy into the performance lie, we place ourselves on that never-ending treadmill. We'll never be able to do enough. Eventually, we lose the joy of our accomplishments because so much pressure comes with them.

Lie 2: *Our self-image depends on the approval of others.* This means we feel good about ourselves only if other people accept us and affirm us. Our personal security can be like a yo-yo, based on how we gauge others' feelings about us.

What about you? To gain approval, you may think you've got to be seen with the right people or wear the right clothes. Or to gain the approval of someone you're dating, you might feel pressured to do something you'll regret.

When I was just beginning to date, I had a huge crush on Bob. One night while we were on a double date, the three of them wanted to go to an X-rated movie on the occult. I was horrified! This was the last film I'd ever intended to see. Although I told Bob I didn't want to go, he and the other couple urged me to go. They said, "What's the harm? Your parents will never know!" Afraid they would think I was weird if I refused, I eventually gave in to their pressure. Because I wanted my boyfriend's approval, I didn't have the courage to firmly state, "No, that's not what I want to do!" I was extremely embarrassed during the film and regretted ever seeing it. That night when I returned home, my dad asked about my evening. With Bob standing there, I burst into tears and confessed about seeing the awful film.

My dad was upset, to say the least. He angrily told Bob that he'd see him later—much later—and ushered him to the door. Then my dad asked me a good question: "Nancy, if you can't say no to a movie, what else can't you say no to?" He was on target.

My infatuation with Bob, and my desire to keep him as a boy-friend, influenced me to compromise my moral convictions.

When we buy into the approval lie, we often compromise our standards because we don't know who we are. Many women allow their "boyfriends" to manipulate and control them, in some cases leading to physical or verbal abuse. Date rape has become a common occurrence, along with other violent treatment. If you've been a victim, you don't have to continue in this pattern. Because the moods, opinions, and values of others are change-able, our self-esteem will be very insecure if we base it on the acceptance and approval of others. Begin to evaluate how guys treat you; it will tell a lot about their character. Get rid of any guy who pushes you beyond your boundaries or encourages you to compromise your values. Focus on developing a healthy self-esteem based on how God feels about you. You are His treasure and deserve to be treated with respect. As you grow in your love relationship with Him, you won't always need a boy-friend to feel good about yourself.

Lie 3: *We must blame others—or ourselves—for our failures.* According to McAllister and McGee, "The problem is that no matter how well we perform or how much approval we gain, all of us will at some time fail. Because we believe that failure dam-ages our self-esteem, we desperately look for some way to mini-mize our mistakes. All too often, our solution is to find some-one to blame."[10]

If you buy into this lie, you're saying that those who fail are unworthy of love and deserve to be punished. By blaming oth-ers—our parents, teachers, coaches, bosses, classmates, friends, even God—we hope to make ourselves feel better. We errone-ously believe the destructive lie that says, "You seem to be better than me, but because you failed and I didn't, I must be superior to you."[11] In reality, this lie doesn't boost our self-worth; it only perpetuates our fear of failure. It also leads us to lie so we will avoid getting into trouble.

When blaming others doesn't work, we blame ourselves. "The act of self-condemnation may be the most severe form of punishment" we ever inflict on ourselves.[12] I can tell you from personal experience that I became my own worst enemy. My mind was constantly bombarded with condemnation. Often, it was vague and carried with it feelings of guilt. Not until I discovered the root of it was I able to counter it with the truth. This lie is very common among women.

Tricia confided in me that she always battled feelings of worthlessness due to her learning disability. She constantly felt she was not good enough and didn't have what it took to measure up. Somehow, she blamed herself, and even blamed God for creating her this way. As we prayed together, confessing the truth of how God sees her, she took a giant step toward changing her destructive mindset.

We need to be released from condemnation with a fresh understanding of God's grace. The truth is that all of us make mistakes and experience failure. God says we are all sinful. Because of that, He knows we will fail. In spite of our failures, God loves us, and He wants us to view our failures as an opportunity to grow. If we've placed our trust in Jesus as our Savior, He assures us, "There is now no condemnation awaiting those who belong to Christ Jesus. For the power of the life-giving Spirit—and this power is mine through Christ Jesus—has freed me from the vicious circle of sin and death" (Romans 8:1,2, TLB). God is more interested in our character than our comfort. He wants to shape our character through our failures, but if we run from them, we will never learn the lessons God has for us.

We need to accept the responsibility for our failures. At those times we need to ask God for His forgiveness, and accept His forgiveness and love. The Bible says, "If we say we have no sin, we are only fooling ourselves and refusing to accept the truth.

But if we confess our sins to him, he is faithful and just to forgive us and to cleanse us from every wrong" (1 John 1:8,9, NLT). As we cooperate with our loving heavenly Father, then our self-esteem will become more what He intends it to be.

Lie 4: *"Shame on me."* This lie says, "There's something wrong with me that can never be repaired." It also says, "I am what I am. I cannot change. I am hopeless."[13] When we buy into this lie, we begin to lower our expectations based on our past failures.

Because I sought the approval of my boyfriend, I compromised my values by watching an X-rated movie with him. It was an occult movie that opened the door to Satan's destructive influence and evil thoughts, and caused me to have frequent nightmares about being sexually abused. Those nightmares always left me feeling shameful and unworthy.

When I was a teenager, the biggest thrill at sleepovers was a seemingly innocent practice of playing with *Ouija* boards. We also played with hypnosis and staged seances to talk with dead spirits. Of course, the negative influences of these practices were not apparent at the time. I now see how dangerous it was to open my mind to Satan's influence.

You may be tempted to view horror movies, experiment with New Age crystals, or dabble in Wicca. These elements of the occult are common, even in today's teen magazines, according to writer Lindy Beam:

> *Teen, Teen People, Seventeen, CosmoGirl!* and *YM* offer monthly horoscope columns. *CosmoGirl!* has featured psychic John Edwards (of TV's "Crossing Over") telling readers how to meditate and use their intuition. In its short lifetime, *Mary-Kate and Ashley* magazine (aimed at preteens) dove into Eastern philosophy, advocating Taoist ideas. Wicca and "goddess spirituality" get occasional nods, too. It's hard to tell whether girls will walk away totally under-

estimating the importance of eternal questions or convinced that they themselves are divine, able to shape their own spiritual destiny.[14]

But beware! Those seemingly harmless activities can open the door to the evil, destructive influences of Satan. The Bible tells us that Satan is a liar (John 8:44) who seeks to destroy our lives through our minds. Unfortunately, we can easily be swayed by his lies, which can lead us to devalue our bodies and the bodies of others.

Many things—being sexually abused, engaging in premarital sex, masturbation, pornography—can cause us shame. In my life, enormous shame and guilt resulted from my eating disorder and sexual compromises. This was destructive until I understood the difference between shame and guilt.

A very helpful description of this difference is found in the *Women's Study Bible:*

> Guilt is a God-given emotion that occurs when a woman's mistakes and faults are brought to her own mind or publicly exposed. Shame, however, says that the person herself is bad, of no value, or unworthy to exist—that she is hopelessly defective, unlovable, inferior, and worthless.
>
> Shame begins externally with a subtle implication through silence and neglect or with verbal denunciation through words of abuse. When such messages are repeated often enough, whether through words or actions, they become internalized into a false belief: I must be bad to deserve such terrible treatment. This becomes the core identity and the basis of thousands of future, flawed choices for the one suffering from shame.
>
> Healing of shame begins when a woman identifies and confesses the lies she has believed about herself. She then must begin to replace those lies with biblical truth about

who God is and who she is as his beloved child—a person of immeasurable worth, righteous and uncondemned.[15]

Guilt is a temporary condition to bring us to repentance before God. Repentance involves being honest with yourself by admitting your sins to God and choosing to turn away from them. With God's help, you can then make lasting changes that will bring healing and health to your physical, emotional, and spiritual life. Once you repent, any guilt or shame that you still feel is not from God.

You may be able to identify with one or more of the lies mentioned in this chapter. During my high school and college years, I experienced the effects of all four of them. I was constantly performing and seeking approval. And with the eating disorder, I blamed myself and felt like a failure, which resulted in tremendous guilt and shame. The only way that I could find my way out of this cycle of despair was to learn to replace the lies I had believed with the truth about God's unconditional, awesome love for me.

> We can easily be swayed by Satan's lies, which can lead us to devalue our bodies.

Think about it. Is it time for you to face reality, too? Which of these lies are you believing? As we continue our journey, this may be the most important step in finding your way to freedom. It begins with learning the truth. Then we can open our hearts to receive true love.

CHAPTER 4

RECEiViNG TRUE LOVE

To face reality, we need to admit that the ideal is unreal. We must be aware of the world's lies about how we should look and perform, and look realistically at our family background and the lies we believe about our self-worth.

Healing from lies about my self-image began when I faced the reality of what was wrong in my life. The eating disorder was merely a symptom of believing wrong things and seeking to satisfy needs in inappropriate ways.

The change came when I asked God for forgiveness and accepted that His Son, Jesus, had died on the cross to pay for my sins. The Bible tells us, "God made Christ, who never sinned, to be the offering for our sin, so that we could be made right with God through Christ" (2 Corinthians 5:21, NLT). What an incredible exchange! All of my imperfections were traded for His perfection.

What freedom to discover that I no longer had to pay for my own sins or try to be perfect! This freedom comes as a result of God's grace. Grace, which is unmerited (unearned) favor, has been described as "God's Riches At Christ's Expense." Grace is the gift of God, which can't be earned, but must merely be received by faith (Ephesians 2:8,9). How amazing God's grace is! At the moment of my decision to accept Christ's forgiveness, I became a new creation through Him; the old passed away and I became new! This transformation is explained in the Bible: "Those who become Christians become new persons. They are not the same anymore, for the old life is gone. A new life has begun!" (2 Corinthians 5:17, NLT). How radically different this was from all of my striving and searching.

My transformation had begun at the popcorn party that night in college. That was the turning point where I placed my trust in Jesus Christ and began to experience new life. But it was just the beginning of an exciting process and a lifetime of growth and change. At that point, I was no longer on my own, trying alone to navigate through my emotions and find a way to cope. Suddenly, with God in my life, I could face the truth and begin to erase the lies I had believed for so many years. In the movie *Ever After*, an updated Cinderella story, we can visualize the radical change needed. How long Cinderella had to listen to demeaning voices and cruel taunts by her stepsisters as she was treated as a slave! Then the prince discovered her and fell in love with her. He rescued her from her bondage, lifting her to royalty. She became a princess, one day to be a queen.

I watched with tears in my eyes the beautiful transformation as she was loved by the prince. What gripped my heart was the real "ideal" we can experience as we receive the true love God wants to pour out on us, as His precious "princesses."

We are now in the transformation process, awaiting our full inheritance as daughters of the King. The Bible describes this transformation:

> Now, the Lord is the Spirit, and wherever the Spirit of the Lord is, he gives freedom. And all of us . . . can be mir-

rors that brightly reflect the glory of the Lord. And as the Spirit of the Lord works within us, we become more and more like him and reflect his glory even more. (2 Corinthians 3:17,18, NLT)

This process is similar to what a caterpillar goes through to become the new creation of a beautiful butterfly. The change is not without struggle, and transformation occurs in definite stages. Let's look at the monarch butterfly as an example. The butterfly's life has four stages: the egg, caterpillar, pupa, and adult. Each stage represents a separate living creature. It is during the pupa stage that the caterpillar undergoes a radical metamorphosis so that it can become a butterfly.

This metamorphosis is not a mere rearrangement of parts, but a complete and fascinating transformation: internal organs of the caterpillar liquefy and are recycled into new tissue; jaws disappear and a specialized tongue appears; short legs are absorbed and new wings are developed.

Just as a butterfly undergoes this transforming process, so it is with us when we begin a relationship with our Creator. The Bible describes our moment of accepting Christ as a rebirth. He gives us a new spirit as well as new internal organs—a new heart and mind—to replace the old ones.

As a child of the King, your transformation can begin with identifying the old belief system and recognizing the lies you've believed about your self-image. Once you identify the lies, you can then replace them with what God says about you, the truth of how He sees and accepts you. You are a Cinderella in process.

Letting Go

Upon confessing my sins and asking God to forgive and heal me, I expected to have no more problems with my eating disorder. I now experienced God's love and forgiveness through Jesus Christ, so I was confused when I fell into the binge-purge cycle again and again. My values had begun to change so that I questioned my involvement in the partying lifestyle, but I loved hanging out with my friends and didn't want to miss the action.

Some nights after a party, I returned home in turmoil over my choices. Turning to food for comfort, I would sneak into the sorority house pantry and stuff myself with any food I could find. Then, feeling remorseful and sick, I'd sneak into the basement bathroom and make myself throw up.

This was the same cycle as before. The only difference was that, as a child of God, I knew I was disappointing Him. Through tears of confusion, I vowed to never do it again. Because I was performance oriented, I determined to overcome the eating disorder like a "good Christian" should. Even so, during my first several months as a Christian, I failed more than ever before. It seemed as if I was failing God. I put great pressure on myself to stop this destructive pattern, but I was fighting against years of bad habits and wrong coping mechanisms.

One night through my tears, I begged God to help me. He led me to 2 Corinthians 12:7–10, where the apostle Paul was pleading with the Lord to remove his "thorn in the flesh." His struggle was different from mine, but God's response to Paul spoke to my situation. Paul tells us, "He said to me, 'My grace is sufficient for you, for my power is made perfect in weakness.' Therefore I will boast all the more gladly about my weaknesses, so that Christ's power may rest on me" (v. 9). At that moment, I saw my weakness in a new light. God could use it to show me His amazing power.

Finally, I realized I could not change on my own, but only through God's grace would I be able to do so. Only by letting go of my own efforts could I experience the grace that had released me from my sins and that could lead me to the freedom God wanted me to experience.

Going back to the butterfly analogy, we can see some more

parallels. Did you know that monarch caterpillars feed exclusively on the poisonous leaves of milkweed plants? This poison varies in strength in each milkweed plant, and remains in the body of the adult butterfly. So by analyzing the poison found in a particular adult monarch butterfly, it's possible to match the poison to the specific type of milkweed plant ingested by the caterpillar.

In much the same way, before we enter a relationship with Christ—during our caterpillar stage—we feed on poisonous lies we've allowed to affect our thinking. And we each have a unique set of lies we believe, just like each butterfly ingests specific poisons of the milkweed plants.

Like the butterfly, my freedom came with discovering the poison that I had fed upon over the years.

The Bible says, "For as [a man] thinks within himself, so he is" (Proverbs 23:7, NASB). This means we each need to take an honest look at ourselves and identify our own wrong patterns of thinking. We need to recognize the faulty thinking we have had, and see our good characteristics the way God sees them.

You Are Designed by God

You may not know what the Bible says about you and how God feels about you, but the ultimate truth is this: God created you exactly as you are, and He loves you more than you can dare to imagine!

The Bible contains a poem about how God created us—you and me! In Psalm 139, the author is talking to God, but God inspired him to write this:

> You created my inmost being; you knit me together in my mother's womb. I praise you because I am fearfully and wonderfully made; your works are wonderful, I know that full well. My frame was not hidden from you when I was made in the secret place. When I was woven together

in the depths of the earth, your eyes saw my unformed body. All the days ordained for me were written in your book before one of them came to be. (Psalm 139:13–16)

Read it again, carefully. This poem reminds me that God is my Creator, and He created my body and soul for a purpose. Believe it or not, He actually chose us "before the creation of the world" (Ephesians 1:4). The Bible also tells us He "predestined us to be adopted as his sons through Jesus Christ, in accordance with his pleasure and will—to the praise of his glorious grace, which he has freely given us in the One he loves" (Ephesians 1:5,6).

> **God wants us to revel in the fact that we are each a unique and special design.**

Understanding this truth is the key to self-acceptance. God fashioned us individually: "With your very own hands you formed me; now breathe your wisdom over me so I can understand you" (Psalm 119:73, *The Message*). His desire was to create someone just like you, and someone just like me. And He will never create another you or another me; we are each unique!

The Bible also tells us "we are God's workmanship, created in Christ Jesus to do good works, which God prepared in advance for us to do" (Ephesians 2:10). Since God created you in your mother's womb, you are His workmanship. Workmanship actually means you are God's *poiema*, which is a Greek word from which the English word "poem" is derived. The word means a work of art or a product that is designed. So you are God's work of art, expressing His thoughts and truths.

Each unchangeable part of you is like a word carefully chosen by a master poet or a color wisely prepared by an artist.

Imagine a canvas with a will of its own, saying to the artist, "I dislike these colors you've painted on me. I reject them." By rejecting the colors, the canvas rejects the message and plan of its designer, rejecting the very purpose for which it exists.

Similarly, you reject your Creator's message and plan for your life if you reject the unchangeable features He's designed specifically for you. Know that from the very moment God had you in His mind, He was an artist creating you unlike anyone else. This means each and every feature, including the size of your frame, your body shape, and your eye color, was designed by God for you.

Some people with larger frames try to have smaller frames; some with brown eyes wish they were blue; some who are short may want to be taller. The story is told of Amy Carmichael, a little girl with brown eyes who always wanted blue. She even prayed that God would change her eye color, but He didn't answer that prayer. You see, what Amy didn't yet know as a little girl was that God had a destiny for her to fulfill in India. Being small with brown hair and brown eyes allowed her to fit in with the culture, where she rescued children from being sold as temple prostitutes. God used Amy in a dramatic and significant way in India, and her physical makeup was part of God's design for her life. He created each individual a certain way for a purpose. He wants us to revel in the fact that we are each His creation—a unique and special design.

Perhaps the greatest happiness in life is to know that we are loved for being ourselves—that our being loved does not depend on what we're trying to be, what we think we should be, or what others want us to be. Only God can love us like that.

For me, great healing and freedom has come from knowing, believing, and remembering this truth daily. In college when I realized the depth of God's love, it changed my whole perspective! I can remember when this really hit me. I would walk around campus thinking, *God loves me. God accepts me. He even delights in me!* Let these words sink into your heart: "The LORD your God is with you, he is mighty to save. He will take great delight in you, he will quiet you with his love, he will rejoice over you with singing" (Zephaniah 3:17). Suddenly it didn't matter what someone else thought about me; I was valuable and special to God! I used to sing songs about God's amazing love for me. Those truths brought joy to my heart and helped me to choose correct thoughts and actions.

God Can Be Your Heavenly Father

Now that you know that God is your Designer and Creator, you can also know Him personally as your heavenly Father. The moment you turn from your sins and place your trust in Jesus, God becomes your "Abba," or Daddy. I love to tell people about my Dad, who runs the universe. You too can know the joy of being a child of God.

> God's Spirit touches our spirits and confirms who we really are. We know who he is, and we know who we are: Father and children. And we know we are going to get what's coming to us—an unbelievable inheritance! We go through exactly what Christ goes through. If we go through the hard times with him, then we're certainly going to go through the good times with him! (Romans 8:16,17, *The Message*)

You can begin to see yourself as God does by understanding His perfect Father-heart. Once you belong to Him, as His dearly loved daughter, He wants to bless you and see you become all He created you to be!

Last year on my spiritual birthday, the day that I celebrate receiving Jesus as my Savior and Lord, I had a huge heavenly hug! My dad surprised me with a dozen red roses. They symbolized so much to me—all that God had done in my life. Not only had He built a deep love relationship with my earthly father (which I'll describe later), but He had shown me His awesome promises of love for me as a perfect heavenly Father.

Whether or not you've ever received a dozen red roses, take a moment and let these twelve incredible promises of God's all-encompassing love touch your heart.

A Dozen Roses of God's Love for You

- *He unconditionally loves you.* "I have loved you with an ever-lasting love; I have drawn you with loving-kindness" (Jeremiah 31:3).

- *He is always with you.* "Where can I go from your Spirit? Where can I flee from your presence? If I go up to the heavens, you are there; if I make my bed in the depths, you are there. If I rise on the wings of the dawn, if I settle on the far side of the sea, even there your hand will guide me, your right hand will hold me fast" (Psalm 139:7–10).

- *He is trustworthy to guide you.* "Trust in the LORD with all your heart; do not depend on your own understanding. Seek his will in all you do, and he will direct your paths" (Proverbs 3:5,6, NLT).

- *He is faithful to forgive you.* "Praise the LORD, I tell myself, and never forget the good things he does for me. He forgives all my sins and heals all my diseases" (Psalm 103:2,3, NLT). See also Psalm 103:10–13.

- *He never changes.* "I will never stop loving him, nor let my promise to him fail. No, I will not break my covenant; I will not take back a single word I said" (Psalm 89:33,34, NLT).

- *He will meet your needs.* "This same God who takes care of me will supply all your needs from his glorious riches, which have been given to us in Christ Jesus" (Philippians 4:19, NLT).

- *He knows your pain.* "The LORD is close to the brokenhearted and saves those who are crushed in spirit" (Psalm 34:18).

- *He delights in you.* "He led me to a place of safety; he rescued me because he delights in me" (Psalm 18:19, NLT).

- *He listens to you.* "The eyes of the LORD watch over those who do right; his ears are open to their cries for help. The LORD hears his people when they call to him for help. He rescues them from all their troubles" (Psalm 34:15,17, NLT).

- *He protects you.* "The LORD is my light and my salvation— so why should I be afraid? The LORD protects me from danger—so why should I tremble?" (Psalm 27:1, NLT).

- *He gives you peace.* "Don't worry about anything; instead, pray about everything. Tell God what you need, and thank him for all he has done. If you do this, you will experience God's peace, which is far more wonderful than the human mind can understand. His peace will guard your hearts and minds as you live in Christ Jesus" (Philippians 4:6,7, NLT).

- *He wants what is best for you.* "'I know the plans I have for you,' declares the LORD, 'plans to prosper you and not to harm you, plans to give you hope and a future'" (Jeremiah 29:11).

Which one of these promises would you like to claim today? I make a habit of hiding these truths in my heart. Because they may take time to sink in, I read them often. As I walk in the morning, I take along index cards on which I've written God's richest promises to meditate on and believe for my need that day.

Meditating on these promises helps us renew our minds with God's truths. You see, we may need some reprogramming.

Wrong perceptions about ourselves may be connected with how our earthly fathers treated us. We may wrongly assume that negative characteristics of our earthly fathers are also true of our heavenly Father. But those are incorrect perceptions of God—He is *all goodness!*

For example, your earthly father may seem distant and uninterested in you. But God is close and always very interested in every detail of your life. Perhaps you felt that your dad was never satisfied with what you did, or he became impatient and angry. But when you are forgiven through Christ, God is pleased with you, and is patient and loving.

Personally, I thought I had to perform for my earthly father. But in my relationship with God, my heavenly Father, I had to learn (and remind myself often) that He loves me as I am and that I don't have to perform for Him in order to receive His love and approval. It's been said that God loves us just as we are, but He loves us too much to leave us that way.

When you are adopted into God's family, you have a completely new identity.

If you truly believe in His Son, you are no longer condemned by God. Believers in Christ can change, because God can change your wrong thoughts and habits, and He can give you a new self-image. *Remember, God's acceptance is the secret to self-acceptance and the end of seeking acceptance from others.*

When you take that step of faith like I did the night of the popcorn party, and accept God's love for you by placing your faith in Jesus Christ, then you become a part of God's family, His very own daughter. When you are adopted into God's family, you have a completely new identity and are transformed, like a caterpillar becoming a butterfly, breaking free to fly!

The more we know about our Creator and God, and His love and acceptance of us, the more we will be able to gladly embrace ourselves and each other, and the less we'll struggle with comparing ourselves to others and striving for perfection and approval.

We've taken a good look at what is real. As we continue our journey, I pray you'll embrace healing for life.

May this poem, written to me by my dad, be symbolic of what your heavenly Father desires for you.

To My Valentine, Nancy

Angels gliding o'er the earth
In splendor thru the skies,
Looking down from high above
With all their sparkling eyes.

Saying that they love you,
How special that you are,
Your face...your heart...your soul,
As bright as any star.

My thoughts of you are just the same.
My heart is light and gay.
Knowing that I love you
More and more each day.

Love, Dad

CHAPTER 5

HEALiNG for LiFE

The purpose in telling my story is to give you hope. If you are battling an eating disorder or any other addictive behavior that is controlling your life, you can be healed! Your yesterdays do not determine your tomorrows. You can be different because God will give you the power to change.

As you've heard through my story, recovery from an eating disorder involves not only physical healing, but also emotional, mental, and spiritual healing. So if you are in the middle of the struggle, don't give up. Put your hope in God, and claim this promise: "May the God of hope fill you with all joy and peace as you trust in him, so that you may overflow with hope by the power of the Holy Spirit" (Romans 15:13).

Many who have placed their trust in Christ have found freedom from an eating disorder. An exchange took place, whereby excessive food and the illusion of control were swapped for God's abundant life. Their emotions became a blessing in their lives instead of a destructive force. Just as countless others have, you too can reach out and receive help.

Sometimes recovering food addicts can learn to help themselves. But in severe cases of eating disorders, it is wise to seek professional help through primary care doctors, psychologists, psychiatrists, registered dietitians, and eating disorder counselors. God uses those professionals to help heal. Regardless of where you seek help, be encouraged to know that over time, healing can occur.

With God's help, you too can be transformed into a beautiful new creation. Returning to the illustration of the monarch, Bill Gothard beautifully describes how the pupa transforms into the butterfly:

> The gold studded turquoise skin (chrysalis) of the monarch pupa becomes transparent after two weeks, making it possible to actually watch the last stages of the metamorphosis of the butterfly. Wings, legs, eyes, and antennae are all visible. During the last few days, cracks spread in the chrysalis wall and allow the butterfly to break free.

This "breaking free" as a new creature is how I felt in my sophomore year of college. I learned that I truly was a "new creation" in Christ. But somehow I was still caught in the cocoon of wrong thinking patterns and a serious case of condemnation and guilt. This shame was a trap for me because I realized how much I'd failed, and it kept me from completely breaking free.

Even though my healing began as soon as I accepted God's love for me through His Son, my "caterpillar thinking" took awhile to break out of the tightly woven cocoon of false security and unhealthy sources of satisfaction. Within about a year of receiving His unconditional love, God healed me of the destructive cycle of bingeing and purging. It was not easy, but as I cooperated with Him in seeing my body as His temple, I asked His Holy Spirit to remind me of that truth. Whenever I was tempted to overeat or make myself sick, I thought of how I would be harming God's temple. The Bible says, "Do you not know that your body is a temple of the Holy Spirit, who is in you, whom you have received from God? You are not your own; you were bought at a price. Therefore honor God with your body" (1 Corinthians 6:19,20). This gave me a new focus for resisting the compulsive behavior. I now belonged to God and He had a plan and purpose for me and my body. Saying no to my addiction was saying yes to God's plan for my life. Although I still failed occasionally and resorted to my old way of coping, I began to forgive myself and move on. During the ups and downs, I saw God shaping me and developing me into His image. Your healing may come quickly or gradually. The time is not as important as the process.

Over time, my old destructive thought patterns have been replaced with new ones.

My healing began as I explored my emotions in a search to discover the source of my pain. Although fearful to face the source of my shame, I discovered that examining the truth brought healing. In facing the truth, I realized I needed to reveal my struggles, repent of my sin, receive God's gift, renew my mind, restore my relationships, and reach out to others.

Over time, my old destructive thought patterns have been replaced with new ones. Yet it is a daily choice to believe and live in the truth of my new identity as God's child. Constantly, I must choose to believe the truth of what God says about me rather than live by my own standards of perfection or the world's standards. This has become easier through the years, but since I am in a continual process of becoming more like God, it is a lifelong transformation.

My old thought patterns occasionally reemerge, tempting

me to use coping mechanisms such as performing for others, relying on achievements for self-worth, or using food as a comfort. Yet, thank God, I have not had a binge-and-purge episode since college. I'm here to tell you there's hope, and to cheer you on in your own journey.

There are six practical guidelines that have helped me heal. Let's start with the first step.

Reveal Your Struggle

Much of life involves a struggle of some sort. It may be a struggle to overcome obstacles in order to achieve, or a struggle to give birth, or for some even a struggle to survive. Don't miss the value of struggles in becoming the person God created you to be.

Again, we can learn from the profound illustration of the butterfly.

A man found a cocoon of a butterfly. One day a small opening appeared. He sat and watched the butterfly for several hours as it struggled to force its body through that little hole. Then it seemed to stop making any progress. It appeared as if it had gotten as far as it could and it could go no further. So the man decided to help the butterfly. He took a pair of scissors and snipped off the remaining bit of the cocoon. The butterfly then emerged easily. But it had a swollen body and small, shriveled wings. The man continued to watch the butterfly because he expected that, at any moment, the wings would enlarge and expand to be able to support the body, which would contract in time.

Neither happened! In fact, the butterfly spent the rest of its life crawling around with a swollen body and shriveled wings. It never was able to fly. What the man in his kindness and haste did not understand was that the restricting cocoon and the struggle required for the butterfly to get through the tiny opening were God's way of forcing fluid from the body of the butterfly into its wings so that it would be ready for flight once it achieved its freedom from the cocoon.[1]

So you see, even though struggles may be painful, they serve a purpose in our lives to make us as strong as God wants us to be. But at the end of every struggle comes the time of healing.

Often healing begins by revealing your struggle and repenting of your sin. Your willingness to admit your problem or weakness to your Creator and to yourself demonstrates that you've faced the truth about yourself. God is all-knowing, but He is waiting for your cooperation in turning the control of your life over to Him. He knows every thought and action you have, but until you admit that your actions are a violation against God, you will continue to try to do things your own way and in your own strength. It wasn't until I came to the end of my own efforts to fix my problem that I could admit I was helpless and turn my struggle over to God.

Repent of Your Sin

As mentioned earlier, repentance is turning away from your sins and turning toward God. It is surrendering control of your own life to Him, and involves a change of mind and heart. When you are faithful to step out in obedience and repentance, God is faithful to transform your heart, mind, and desires.

Before and during my eating disorder, I struggled with negative thinking. I would often have thoughts like, *You could never do that. You're not good enough. Look at you—who do you think you are?*

As I sought healing, one of the first things I did was confess to God the wrongness of my eating disorder and my negative thoughts. I needed to ask God's forgiveness for not caring about my body and not accepting myself. I said to God, "Please forgive me for abusing my body. Please forgive me for beating myself up with wrong thoughts about myself."

In faith and prayer, I turned away from this sin, and surrendered to Him the control of my life. Admitting that I was helpless to change myself, I was finally free to let Him work in me. This began a process whereby I cooperated with God's transforming power.

I needed to replace those negative thoughts with the truth of what God says about me. I realized that I was my own worst enemy, especially when I constantly blamed myself and then wallowed in guilt. These destructive thought patterns were based on a faulty view of myself. I had a sense of condemnation so that no matter how much I did, I was never good enough. These thoughts were rooted in a prideful drive to perpetuate the idea that I could attain perfection on my own. I realized not only that they were lies, but also that I was sinning by believing them and allowing them to continue to swim around in my head. God wants us to take those negative thoughts captive.

I learned to substitute a negative mindset for a positive one and to "practice praise." It took my mind off my inadequacies and onto God's sufficiency. The Bible tells us how we can renew our minds: "Summing it all up, friends, I'd say you'll do best by filling your minds and meditating on things true, noble, reputable, authentic, compelling, gracious—the best, not the worst; the beautiful, not the ugly; things to praise, not things to curse" (Philippians 4:8, *The Message*).

Receive God's Gift

Do you want to experience God's grace and receive His forgiveness and cleansing? Are you ready to release control of your life to Him? Can you admit, "God, I need you; I want you to heal me"? If you have never received Jesus Christ as your personal Savior, this is your invitation. Jesus says, "Yet to all who received him, to those who believed in his name, he gave the right to become children of God" (John 1:12).

He loves us so much that He gave His life to purchase our forgiveness with His own blood. His love is freely given, but as with any love relationship, the one pursued has the choice to respond or reject the lover. The Lover of your soul knocks at the door of your heart: "Here I am! I stand at the door and knock. If anyone hears my voice and opens the door, I will come in and eat with him, and he with me" (Revelation 3:20). How you respond to His invitation will determine your destiny, both here and in eternity. Only Jesus can cleanse your of your sins and bring you into a relationship with God. Only Jesus can satisfy your deepest longings and desires. He has created you for Himself and wants you to spend eternity with Him.

If you aren't sure whether you are a new creation in Christ, you can be "born again" today as God's child. Jesus declared to Nicodemus, a very religious man, "I tell you the truth, no one can see the kingdom of God unless he is born again" (John 3:3). This seemed impossible to Nicodemus, but Jesus explained what it meant: "Humans can reproduce only human life, but the Spirit gives new life from heaven" (John 3:6, NLT). Jesus was referring to a spiritual birth, which gives us a new beginning.

This is the miracle of new birth in Christ. He wants you to become a member of God's family, a child of the heavenly Father.

You can simply express your desire to God in prayer. He already knows your heart. Prayer is simply reaching out in faith to receive His gift of forgiveness. If you would like to receive this gift, pray a prayer like this one from your heart:

"Lord Jesus, I need you. I admit that I have sinned against you, and I am sorry. Thank You for dying on the cross in my place to rescue me from the penalty of my sins. I trust in You, and I open the door of my life and receive You as my Savior and Lord. Thank You for forgiving me of my sins and giving me eternal life. Take control of the throne of my life and make me the kind of person You want me to be."

Dear friend, pause right now and make this your own prayer. If you sincerely turn control of your life over to Christ, He will come into your life as He promised. You will now have the power of God to overcome any obstacles to healing. The Christian life is "Christ in you." He will live His life through your body, guiding and strengthening you, and you will have a new identity as a child of God:

> How great is the love the Father has lavished on us, that we should be called children of God! And that is what we are!...Dear friends, now we are children of God, and what we will be has not yet been made known. But we know that when he appears, we shall be like him, for we shall see him as he is. Everyone who has this hope in him purifies himself, just as he is pure. (1 John 3:1–3)

I have found it life-changing to focus on who I am as a Christian. In Appendix C I've included a list, developed by Freedom in Christ Ministries, which you may want to use each day for the next month to discover your identity as a believer in Christ.

Your Personal Counselor

To help you through your struggles and guide you each day, God has provided your own personal Counselor as a gift. Before Jesus left the earth, He said to His followers, "I will ask the Father, and he will give you another Counselor to be with you forever—the Spirit of truth...The Counselor, the Holy Spirit, whom the Father will send in my name, will teach you all things and will remind you of everything I have said to you" (John

14:16,17,26). The Holy Spirit actually lives within you, providing help, comfort, and encouragement, and teaching you about God.

What a committed coach and instructor He is! I take a kick-boxing class that often reminds me of the Holy Spirit's role in my life. My coach, Nelson, is always telling me to breathe: to exhale the impure air and inhale fresh air. This is similar to a concept called Spiritual Breathing, taught by Dr. Bill Bright, in which we exhale by confessing sin and inhale by receiving God's forgiveness and cleansing. Nelson pushes me to kick harder, strengthening my muscles (developing my faith) and fighting against my opposition (the devil and his lies).

Are you ready to sign up? Whether you're in kick-boxing or not, you are in God's spiritual training class. Thankfully He is a patient, persistent teacher!

Late one evening at a fraternity party, after I had given my life to Jesus, I found myself a little tipsy. Still wanting to run my own life, I thought I'd be an example at the kegger. So with a "Bible in one hand and a beer in the other" (not exactly—I drank wine and didn't carry my Bible), I tried to let my light shine and be His witness.

> **God had my attention—my strategy to run my own life was not working.**

It was late, and I had taken my contact lenses out, creatively (I thought) putting them in two cups on the fireplace. To my dismay, when I went to retrieve them, I discovered that someone had apparently drank my lenses! God had my attention—my strategy to run my own life was not working. I felt like a failure as a witness and as a Christian. I was now primed to give up my own efforts to live the Christian life and allow Jesus Christ to live through me. I learned that it's impossible for anyone to live the Christian life; only Jesus Christ can live it through it through us as we allow His Spirit to have control of our lives.

The Bible tells us, "Do not get drunk on wine, which leads to debauchery. Instead, be filled with the Spirit" (Ephesians 5:18). I knew what it meant to be drunk, so now I was beginning to learn about giving the Holy Spirit the controlling power in my life. To be filled with, or controlled by, the Holy Spirit is God's command. He has also given us this promise: "This is the confidence we have in approaching God: that if we ask anything according to his will, he hears us. And if we know that he hears us —whatever we ask—we know that we have what we asked of him" (1 John 5:14,15). God assures us that when we ask Him to fill us with His Spirit, He will answer our prayer. Do you desire to be filled with the Holy Spirit? You may wish to stop right now and pray, asking God to fill you with His Holy Spirit and to control your life.

Next to receiving Jesus as my Savior, understanding the Holy Spirit's role in helping me overcome my struggle has been the most incredible truth. Jesus actually lives within every Christian and has given His Spirit to guide our lives. So rather than trying to control everything on my own, I can let go and trust that God can give me victory as I yield control of my life to Him.

How is this possible? You can simply invite the Holy Spirit to fill you, asking Him to mold you and shape you to honor Him through your body.

What a liberating truth to realize that God has purchased you and you belong to Him! You are not your own, but you have been bought with a price—the precious blood of Jesus. So as He takes responsibility for your body, you can relax knowing that He is in the struggle with you and is committed to making you all that He created you to be. In response to God's forgiveness and His incredible love for us, He wants us to offer our lives and our bodies to Him: "Therefore, I urge you, brothers, in view of God's mercy, to offer your bodies as living sacrifices, holy and pleasing to God—this is your spiritual act of worship. Do not conform any longer to the pattern of this world, but be transformed by the renewing of your mind. Then you will be able to test and approve what God's will is—his good, pleasing and perfect will" (Romans 12:1,2). That brings us to the next step—renewing the mind.

Renew Your Mind

A major factor in my healing was the process of replacing wrong thinking about my self-image, my body, and my circumstances. I had to work to "renew my mind" with healthy thoughts. Renewing your mind doesn't happen immediately. Sarah Ferguson relates her struggle to change her thought patterns:

> [She] admits, "As a grown woman I was virtually blind to the triggers that would set me off on a binge." Those triggers—feelings of low self-esteem, abandonment, loneliness and stress (experienced both when her mother and Prince Andrew left)—are issues many people face when confronting habitual overeating... "I had reached a point in my life where I was plain unhappy with myself," she now says. "I felt overwhelmed and it showed in my weight, home life, finances and attitude. A structured diet like Weight Watchers' taught me how to see food in context and getting into a fitness regimen elevated my mood... There are good days and bad days. Food is always going to be an issue for me. But I've learned to be patient and honest with myself. And if I fall off my diet, I know how to get back on track without beating myself up."[2]

You can make great strides in renewing your mind and in changing your habits through the help of a friend, talking with a good counselor, attending a Christian church, studying the

Bible with others, and reading insightful books. But be careful who you allow to influence your thinking. Make sure you are receiving truth to replace the lies. For some great resources to get you started, see Appendix B.

My new way of thinking helped me understand that my body belonged to God. Soon, I began to consider how to honor my body rather than destroy it. As I did that, I saw my weight in a whole new light. I began thinking "healthy" versus "skinny." Don't get me wrong—I still wanted to be in good shape. That goal is okay as long as I view my body from God's perspective and not the world's. Now I'm highly motivated to be in good shape, but for a different reason than when I was bulimic. I desire to glorify God with my body and be a picture frame for Jesus. Rather than drawing attention to my body, I want to represent my King well! We need to have good health and energy to fulfill God's purpose for our lives.

On the practical level, my wardrobe needed renovation also. As women we like to make the most of our God-given assets through our attire, but I never realized how this affected men until a guy friend of mine told me, "Nancy, your blouse is causing me problems!"

"What are you talking about?" I naively asked.

He explained how guys are affected strongly by what they see. Wow! I had never thought of it that way! I just wanted to look nice and thought the blouse looked good.

So I had a choice to make: Do I go along with the world's standards and display everything I've got, or do I choose to honor God in the way I dress?

After I became a Christian, I decided that some of my sorority sisters would like my sexy clothes, and I could buy new ones. So the sign went up: Clothes for Sale. You can imagine the conversations this sparked!

Over the years, I have discovered that it's possible to dress modestly while still making the most of my physical assets. Instead of highlighting my body, I can look attractive by accenting my unique shape, coloring, and taste. With the help of my nieces, I stay in style!

Another benefit of my new way of thinking was that I began to focus on what is true about myself and others. The truth of the Bible became the source of my belief system instead of relying solely on my feelings. Jesus tells us that if we follow the teachings in the Bible, "You will know the truth, and the truth will set you free" (John 8:32).

If truth is what sets us free, then lies keep us in bondage. If we believe a lie as truth, it will affect our lives as if it were true, even though it is a lie. And after awhile, lies begin to sound like the truth and the truth sounds like lies.

Renewing the mind is hard work, so we can't give up. God will help, but the process is demanding. To get rid of the lies, we need to use the eject button on the tape player of our minds. Then we need a new tape to record on our minds the truth of who we are in Christ—God's child who is dearly loved, fully accepted, and completely forgiven.

We also need to throw away the distorting fun-house mirror and the magnifying mirror. Instead, we must pick up the true mirror of God's Word and begin seeing ourselves through His eyes.

To find the truth about you, start by reading and meditating on Psalm 139 in the Bible. You can find other truths by reading the list in Appendix C of this book. Once you know the truth, play the tape of God's truth repeatedly in your mind.

Another great way to learn God's truth is to get involved in a Bible study with others. My Christian friends and I started a Bible study in my sorority house and, believe it or not, they voted me chaplain for the house.

On my twenty-first birthday, my sorority sisters all wanted

me to go to a bar to celebrate! Instead, I invited them to the river to watch my baptism. I'll never forget the look on their faces. Later, several of them came to know Jesus personally and joined us in our Bible study. They had observed the changes in my life, and were drawn to the One who was responsible.

Little did I know that the Lord was preparing me for a future in full-time ministry. I began to share what God had done in my life with others who also needed to know His freedom and grace.

My desire to share this life-changing message with others continued to grow. I thought of all my friends in high school who struggled with similar problems. Maybe I could help reach high school students who are making choices that will affect them the rest of their lives.

> Another key element in my healing process was restoring a relationship.

I sensed God calling me to invest my life in young people. I discovered that Campus Crusade for Christ had a high school ministry called Student Venture.

When I told my parents about my desire, they were not thrilled, to say the least. This was all new to them and wasn't exactly what they had envisioned for my life. After many tears and discussions, they released me to follow God's path for my life.

Their approval had always been a tremendous motivation in my life, so the fact that I was able to choose for myself was a huge step of growth for me. They eventually came to embrace my mission and support me in it. We have grown together through the process.

Several years later, after a period with numerous speaking

engagements, I was wiped out! I had pushed myself to the limit and had a physical breakdown. I literally had to be helped off the plane on my way home from Russia. My vocal chords were also in serious jeopardy, so the doctor prescribed "rest and no talking."

Through God's amazing grace, I ended up at Canaan in the Desert, a place of rest I mentioned earlier. At the retreat center was a counselor and representative from the Freedom in Christ Ministries. She prayed with me for healing, both physical and emotional. Through an emotional "melt-down," I got to the root of some deep pain. It allowed me to face areas of my life where I'd tried to apply Band-Aids instead of performing radical surgery.

Upon her recommendation, I attended a conference by Freedom in Christ Ministries where I benefited greatly from working through Dr. Neil Anderson's "Seven Steps to Freedom." Going through the steps with the help of a prayer counselor, God revealed to me some ways I had allowed my beliefs to be corrupted so that strongholds could take root in my mind. A stronghold is anything in my life that has a "strong hold" on me, which controls my behavior. As I confessed these strongholds to God and began to face reality, I experienced new levels of healing and freedom. Overwhelmed by God's love that is so compassionate and accepting, my "caterpillar thinking" was beginning to be transformed with my Creator's thinking.

Restore Broken Relationships

Another key element for me in the healing process was restoring a relationship. Although my relationship with my dad wasn't broken, I had never been honest with him about the expectations I thought he had of me.

One Christmas about ten years after college, I was visiting my family in St. Louis. I had been battling those same throat problems that resulted in vocal nodules. Not being able to speak for several months had revealed that I still had some performance issues. I realized how closely my identity was tied to my performing and accomplishing. That night, I felt completely worthless after one more setback in my healing led to my inability to do anything in my ministry. I cried uncontrollably as one of my brothers held me. For the first time, I was able to be real with my family. I told my brother and dad how I had always felt pressured to perform and to live up to the image of "having it all together."

It seemed God had orchestrated that experience to give me an opportunity to let my dad know how I felt all those years. He was so touched. Tears welled up in his eyes as he said, "I didn't ever mean for you to feel that way." We hugged and experienced a new level of understanding that night. God had prepared my dad's heart, because he also had come to have a personal relationship with Jesus. He was now freer to express his emotions.

There was a process to bring our communication to that level. Be prepared, as you confront your loved ones, that they may not understand or respond in such a gracious way. They may be defensive or refuse to take responsibility. But remember that your heavenly Father cares, and He is holding your hand, guiding you. Keep trusting Him no matter what. Praying for your parents and family will strengthen you in your journey and allow God to work in your situation.

When issues are brought into the light, the truth can shine on them. That conversation with my family brought such healing to me as the truth was revealed. It enabled me to be real with them. I no longer thought I needed to hide my feelings. In fact, being honest with my struggles and emotions brought us closer together. It also enabled me to relate what God had done in my heart. By God's grace, over time my five siblings and both parents have given their lives to Jesus and been born spiritually into God's family. What broken relationships in your life need to be restored with the truth?

Perhaps you are longing to experience understanding in your relationship with your father. If you are unable to know that your father loves and accepts you, you can be sure that your heavenly Father is your Daddy. He can fill your longing for love in ways that are humanly impossible.

Maybe you need to forgive someone who's hurt you. Often the most destructive poison in our lives is our own bitterness. Forgiveness happens when anger and bitterness are replaced with God's love. God tells us we can forgive because He has forgiven us. If your heart is walled up with bitterness or unforgiveness, you can choose to let go of the offense and forgive. You forgive, not because others deserve it, but because you want to be free to become everything God created you to be. Forgiving others does not mean they will be free from the consequences of their sin; it just leaves the responsibility of judging them to God, and He will do a much better job of it. Remove those barriers for your own sake. It's what God wants you to do, and it will allow you to experience God's Father-love for you. Take a moment now and ask God to bring to your mind those who have hurt you or disappointed you.

In her book *A Woman's Search for Worth*, Dr. Deborah Newman provides some excellent insights and describes the healing power of forgiveness.

> For deep offenses, it may take years to experience the full freedom of forgiveness. I compare forgiveness to peeling layers off an onion. You can dig deeply and take off many layers at once, but there are lots of thin layers as well, which makes forgiveness a process of patiently addressing the issues that come up.
> - Is God speaking to you about forgiving a certain person?

- Are you willing to commit to the process?

Committing to the process means admitting that you are powerless to forgive on your own. You are telling God that you want Him to forgive in you. You are willing to begin, knowing it may take years before you feel the complete release of God's work of forgiveness in your heart.[3]

Dr. Newman describes three stages that can help guide you through the process of forgiveness:

1. Fully examine the wrong. A lot of us don't experience the full healing power of forgiveness because our spirituality won't allow us to feel the anger that is stored inside. Ephesians 4:26 says to be angry and sin not. Anger in itself is not sin. It is what we do with our anger that makes it sin. I find it helpful to express the anger in my soul in a letter that I don't send to the person who offended me. This helps me fully recognize the reality of who and what God is asking me to forgive.

2. Confess your own sins. How have you allowed the sin committed against you to influence you to sin? Have you been angry at God? Have you developed a life of hate and anger? Have you become afraid to live? Have you not loved well? Have you been afraid to love God? It is important for you to honestly admit your own sins and take responsibility for your own life in the process of forgiveness.

3. Commit to the process of forgiveness. Now it's time to let God do what only He can do. Forgiveness in the Spirit is a spiritual process. He can reach and cleanse places in your soul that you could never touch. It's time to trust God and let Him free you from the bondage of unforgiveness.

True forgiveness is one of the most important instructions Jesus gives us. The reality of a fallen world makes forgiveness the only true remedy for the damage done to our souls by hurtful relationships. I challenge you to consider the deep work of forgiveness and let God know that you are willing to practice true forgiveness in your relationship. As you practice true forgiveness, you are well on your way toward ending your cycle of damaging relationships.[4]

Once you have restored broken relationships in your life, you will experience a new freedom to build healthy relationships.

Reach Out to Others

Healing has also come to me as I have reached out to others. Reaching out involves not only telling another person about my struggles, but also learning to be a real friend to someone else. It means putting other people before myself and truly caring about them.

Telling someone about my eating disorder was a big step in my healing process. About a year after I became a Christian, I attended a weekend retreat with other college students. I had kept my problem a secret for so long, but for some reason, I really wanted to tell my friend Vickie about my struggle. The amazing thing is that, of all the girls there, Vickie also struggled with an eating disorder. We confided in each other, cried together, prayed for each other, and became good friends. After sharing with Vickie, it became easier to confide in others. I had some friends who helped me through their counsel in God's Word, accountability, and prayer. After blowing it one day, I remember riding my bike over to their house with tears streaming down my cheeks. "Could God ever forgive me for all my failures?" I sobbed. They gently pointed me to God's Word to encourage me about His loving acceptance and grace. The Bible says, "If we are faithless, he will remain faithful, for he cannot disown himself" (2 Timothy 2:13).

Their hugs, prayers, and understanding freed me to pick myself up and keep going. Whenever I felt tempted, I knew I could call them for counsel and prayer. My bingeing and purging episodes gradually lessened, and by the end of the year I was freed from the destructive cycle!

If you are struggling with an eating disorder, drinking too much, sexual promiscuity, self-image problems, jealousy, anger, or anything else, I urge you to confide in a trusted friend. Find someone to share your struggle with and to hold you accountable for making healthy choices. Be honest with her; let her know when you mess up and how she can pray for you.

Find someone to hold you accountable for making healthy choices.

The Bible tells us to confess our sins to each other and pray for each other so that we will be healed (James 5:16). As we do this, we need to accept each other unconditionally, just as God accepts us—no requirements, no strings attached. Within an honest relationship, your friend can point you to God and you can do the same for her. Remind each other of God's truth about you, and together reject the world's lies.

For some, the struggle is so great that they need to talk with a professional counselor. This was true for me. If it were not for the help of some mature counselors, I would never have been able to get to the root of my problem and find healing. Although healing is a process, these ABCs of self-acceptance, distilled from their advice, may be helpful for you to begin focusing on.

A—Accept yourself as unique and special.
Begin to believe what God says about you as opposed to what others may think. Through joining a small group Bible study, I

learned more about God's great, awesome love for me. I remember asking the leader, "What about drinking and partying and going with boys who do? And what about being outspoken? I'm not very quiet and reserved." Basically, I was struggling with a certain image that I thought I had to fulfill now that I was a Christian.

Her answered surprised and liberated me. She said, "Nancy, make your goal to fall in love with Jesus and He will fashion you into His unique image."

I could handle that. Falling in love with Jesus was easy! He is so incredible and incomparably awesome and intimate in His love. As I learned more about Him from the Bible, His love filled the deepest needs in my heart and soul.

My identity began to be rooted in how God felt about me. I was His unique design, and I didn't have to produce a certain "behavior" or "image." I just needed to allow Him to live through my personality and design. This truth began to free me from condemnation, comparison, and competition.

You and I are His creative creations, designed to show His beauty in a one-of-a-kind way! You are special to Him and hold a place in His heart that is for you alone! Understanding this revelation will release you from the limitations you place on yourself.

B—Be a friend who encourages and believes in others.
As you reach outside of yourself and begin to look at the needs of those around you, you will find a security growing within. Your focus becomes what it should be: more others-centered and less self-centered. I even started leading a small group Bible study with several friends, one of whom struggled with an eating disorder, too. As I counseled my friend, I grew in confidence. The more we rehearse these truths to others, the more they are cemented in our hearts and minds.

Remember, a pivotal key to healing is to reach out to others. God will often use our weaknesses to reveal His power. God has used the very thing I've struggled with the most to help me reach out to others and lead them to healing. Our pain often becomes our platform to help others. In turn, that reaching out has played a role in my own transformation into His image.

C—Change your focus.

Focus on your character rather than your image. Image is only exterior; character is interior, the place where true beauty shines forth. God's Word tells us what's truly important: "Charm is deceptive, and beauty is fleeting; but a woman who fears the LORD is to be praised" (Proverbs 31:30). As you focus on building character qualities, you will find a new sense of self-confidence based on discovering the gifts God gave you to contribute to the lives of others. Realize that the challenges you are in the process of overcoming are the tools God will use to shape you to fulfill His purpose for your life. When the Lord was choosing a king for Israel, the prophet Samuel thought it would be an outwardly handsome one. But God told Samuel, "Do not consider his appearance or his height, for I have rejected him. The LORD does not look at the things man looks at. Man looks at the outward appearance, but the LORD looks at the heart" (1 Samuel 16:7). David, the man God chose as king, was later called "a man after God's own heart."

God is looking at your heart today. Make your focus to please and honor Him. He rewards those who seek Him!

The ABCs of self-acceptance can be challenging because our world rewards image and external success. But as we begin to learn about who God is and His incredible love for us, we will desire to choose what God values and loves, which ultimately brings true satisfaction and happiness in life. Letting go of our control in exchange for Him controlling our life is the only path to true freedom and contentment.

I've recently completed a weekend conference for college and high school girls where these issues were addressed. During our last session one precious girl, Amber, opened up about her three-year struggle with bulimia. Together we gathered around her, prayed for her, and she in turn confessed her sin and desperate need for deliverance from this bondage. She renounced her addiction and announced to the Lord her desire to obey Him and discover His way of living in a less than ideal world.

Two of Amber's friends committed to an accountability relationship with her where they would meet together once a week. All three have struggled in this area and together decided to do a Bible study I had written, *Chosen With a Mission*, as well as seek counseling.

The change in Amber's life was remarkable. There was a hope restored and a new course charted. With the help of the Holy Spirit and committed friends, she's on the path to healing. Wherever you find yourself on your journey, you can be assured that, ideal or not, you too can have victory over your challenges.

The following poem, by Dr. Warren Wiersbe, struck me as a great summary of our position in God's family and the power He has to transform lives. I hope it encourages and inspires you as it has me.

> When the child of God
> Looks into the Word of God
> And sees the Son of God
> (S)he is changed by the Spirit of God
> Into the image of God
> For the glory of God.

CHAPTER 6

iDEAL or NOT

Angel caught my attention immediately. She was a beautiful young African woman sitting across the crowded restaurant. Swaziland is bush country, but it does have Kentucky Fried Chicken. After a long week of ministering in the village, hospitals, train station, and high schools, I considered a visit to "the Colonel" a treat!

After enjoying my meal, I went over to meet this striking young woman. She introduced herself as Angel. "What a charming name for a beautiful young woman," I said.

As we got acquainted, I discovered that *she was married to the prince!* Wow! A royal princess eating at KFC! Knowing the reality of life in African culture, I asked her what it was like to be married to the prince. She replied that things were going well; her husband had only one wife for now. (Usually, they take several.)

She asked me, "Do you have a husband?"

"No," I answered.

She looked concerned for me. In Africa, being a single woman is not so cool! I assured her that I was very happy being single.

As we got to know each other better, we seemed to connect. She then looked up with bright eyes and asked, "If my husband proposed to you, would you marry him?"

Wow! No one had ever offered me their husband before. I smiled. This was a first.

"Thank you so much for offering, Angel, but no thanks. You see, I may not be married, but I do have a Prince. His name is Jesus. Have you ever met Him?"

She knew some facts about Jesus, but she didn't know Him personally. In the next moments, I had the privilege of introducing Angel to her true Prince—the One who gave His life for her.

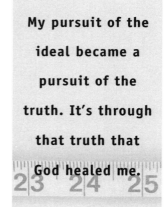

My pursuit of the ideal became a pursuit of the truth. It's through that truth that God healed me.

You see, even if we don't have the ideal Prince on this earth, we are princesses of the royal King of heaven. Our passion for perfection is rooted in our eternal destiny. We are made for Him and, whether we consider ourselves ideal or not, He loves us and wants us to live forever with Him.

My journey has now taken me all over the world. Living "on the edge" has been beyond my imagination. God promises to do more than we can imagine when we turn our lives over to Him: "No eye has seen, no ear has heard, no mind has conceived what God has prepared for those who love him" (1 Corinthians 2:9).

I started out pursuing the ideal—the ideal body, the ideal boyfriend, the ideal life. My search took me through some painful places and brought me to the end of myself. It was then that I realized I was being pursued by the Lover of my soul. I found a new life in Christ through a relationship with Him.

With my heavenly Father's help, I was able to see what is real. The lies I had believed were unveiled, and I saw my family relationships and myself in a new light: through God's eyes. My pursuit of the ideal became my pursuit of the truth. It's through that truth that God healed me.

I have been given the gift of freedom from my sin and bondage. I've lived an incredible life as I've flown all over the world through my ministry, speaking to high school and college students as well as women of all ages. Little did I know that my pain would become my platform. It's been an exciting adventure, daring to be real!

Know that God has great plans for you, as well. God created you with a personal uniqueness, specific personality traits, skills, abilities, and gifts, put together to make you individually distinct. If you have trusted His Son, Jesus, you are now a daughter of our heavenly Father. And as a child of the King of the universe, you are a princess and have been given incredible privileges and benefits. But it doesn't stop there.

The most amazing truth is that you are also a "bride." Jesus refers to all true believers as His bride; together we make up the bride of Christ. What delightful thoughts come to your mind as you picture yourself as a "bride"? Countless women have expressed to me their desire to be a bride and told me of creative plans for their wedding day. Guys can't relate as well to this image, but they can understand the unique role of being a bride. Disney offers a fairy-tale wedding package for anyone who can afford it (just like Cinderella)! But who can compare with the King of glory preparing a wedding banquet for His bride? We are offered a glimpse of that glorious day:

> Then I heard what sounded like a great multitude, like the roar of rushing waters and like loud peals of thunder, shouting: "Hallelujah! For our Lord God Almighty reigns.

Let us rejoice and be glad and give him glory! For the wedding of the Lamb has come, and his bride has made herself ready. Fine linen, bright and clean, was given her to wear." (Fine linen stands for the righteous acts of the saints.) (Revelation 19:6–8)

This revelation has filled me with wonder and captivated my imagination. I believe the Lord uses this imagery to reveal the depth of His desire for us to know Him intimately, and to communicate the intensity of His passionate love for us! The summation of all history will culminate with a wedding celebration. We are now being prepared as His bride.

In the Book of Isaiah, we can discover more of this truth: "You will be a crown of splendor in the Lord's hand, a royal diadem in the hand of your God...As a bridegroom rejoices over his bride, so will your God rejoice over you" (Isaiah 62:3,5).

As we look at one final glimpse from the heart of our Father and Bridegroom, we are encouraged to forget the past and embrace our future. Picture Him speaking to you as His beloved daughter and bride as you read this wedding psalm:

Listen, O daughter, consider and give ear: Forget your people and your father's house *(let go of your past)*. The king is enthralled by your beauty *(receive His view of you)*; honor him, for he is your lord *(look to His approval alone)*. The Daughter of Tyre will come with a gift, men of wealth will seek your favor. All glorious is the princess within her chamber; her gown is interwoven with gold *(the King sees you as pure and holy because of the blood of Jesus)*. In embroidered garments she is led to the king *(He's given you a new wardrobe—a garment of salvation and a robe of righteousness)*; her virgin companions follow her and are brought to you *(you will be an example to others)*. They are led in with joy and gladness; they enter the palace of the king. (Psalm 45:10–15, commentary added)

This vividly portrays our new identity as seen by the Lover of our souls, the One who has pursued us from the beginning of time. With eager anticipation, we can joyfully await our eternal destiny, while living out fully our purpose to glorify Jesus now.

You are His special treasured possession in whom He delights. Every woman desires to be chosen and cherished, and every man desires honor and respect. Knowing your value and worth, both now and eternally, will revolutionize your life. You have been chosen by the Lord for His pleasure and glory: "'You are my witnesses,' declares the LORD, 'and my servant whom I have chosen, so that you may know and believe me and understand that I am he. Before me no god was formed, nor will there be one after me'" (Isaiah 43:10). Your journey in this life is a quest to know the Lord Jesus and to make Him known.

If you have been born again and have begun a personal relationship with Jesus Christ, you have a completely new identity, just like a butterfly! The next time you see a butterfly in all its beauty, sailing along on the wind, remember that God desires freedom, joy, and spontaneity in your life. Let the problems of your life motivate you to continue to seek Him and His answers.

You have been chosen by God for a very special purpose and plan that only you can fulfill. I have written another book called *Chosen With a Mission*, with a companion Bible study, which could help you establish these truths firmly in your life and embrace your mission. Wherever you are on your journey, God is with you to guide your next step. He will lead you in this adventure as you lay aside *your* ideal and take up *His* ideal.

It's been said that a monarch butterfly can cover more than 650 miles without landing. Who knows the miles you will travel as you learn to fly in freedom with Jesus. He alone can release you from your bondage and set you on a new flight path. I encourage you to be the beautiful butterfly He created you to be. Remember, you were born to fly! Imagine the possibilities!

Taking Flight

On the wings of your Spirit I fly,
All my own efforts now die;

The cry of my heart is You,
Who alone makes me new;

Heavenly vinedresser I wait,
Forgive me if I hesitate;

Take Your shears to prune,
Prepare me for Your coming soon;

Make me full and fruitful,
Cleanse away the dull;

Let my fruit bring You joy,
With no hidden alloy;

A butterfly that's free,
Unencumbered as can be;

Abiding in You, my treasure,
Soaring without measure.

Heavenly Father, thank You for the way You have made me. I especially thank You for those unchangeable features that at times I have resented. I accept them now as marks of Your ownership to remind me daily that You made me and that I belong to You. I also welcome them as motivation to develop Your character within me. I want to receive the gift of Your grace and acceptance of me as demonstrated through Jesus dying to free me from my sin and my expectations to be perfect. There is no one ideal but You. And ideal or not, I am accepted by You—just as I am. I thank You for this gift, and I ask You to give me the full measure of freedom for which You created me. Amen.

APPENDIX A

ASK an EXPERT

I n hopes of addressing some questions you may have about eating disorders, included is a brief interview with Kelly V. Bauer, LPC, NCC, a therapist with New Life Clinics in St. Louis, Missouri.

What are the key contributing factors in developing an eating disorder?
I believe there are several contributing factors, but I'll mention three (not placed in any particular order):

1. The "bent" of the person or the person's God-given temperament/personality plays a role. For example, some folks lean naturally towards a "perfectionist" mode in life. The standard of perfectionism can certainly make life stressful. I have worked with a substantial number of women with eating disorders who have this tendency.

2. Family dynamics can play a significant role in the etiology (origin) of an eating disorder. This is not to place blame on parents or family; blame-placing has no benefit for a patient.

To look and explore how the family "operated" or functioned helps us understand the depth of feelings, misunderstandings, or hurts, and allows for us, with the help of Jesus, to move beyond these hurts.

3. Eating disorders may start out legitimately as health issues or losing weight. With many women, beliefs about themselves in terms of their value and worth may have a great influence in this. A woman may have an image of her body that is negative or "distorted." These beliefs about herself can significantly impact the process of losing weight or dieting, many times propelling it out of control, creating depression or an increase in depression and anxiety. This can become a vicious cycle, decreasing self-esteem, and increasing the distortion or the perception of the body.

Please note: Many times a woman will set a goal weight of x number of pounds. When she achieves this weight, she may continue to reset the goal, which becomes unrealistic. As restriction or purging of food continues, depression increases and the ability to be logical/rational decreases. This is the time when friends and family need to step in lovingly, firmly, and supportively to help.

How important are family dynamics?
I touched on this in the first question. Let me continue by saying it's important in families to have structure and rules. Yet the goal for all families is to find the balance of love and structure. It is important to allow for flexibility when possible. I support what two helpful Christian psychologists (Dr. Randy Carlson and Dr. Kevin Leman) have encouraged in their ministry, "Rules With Relationship." Relationship is so precious. Building, establishing, and maintaining it in the family is vital, just as developing our relationship with our heavenly Father is vital!

Ask an Expert

Have you identified a process for healing someone struggling with an eating disorder?
As I work with someone with an eating disorder, one of my primary initial objectives is to make sure they are stable physically. I encourage a visit to their primary care physician. Their doctor should check their electrolyte and iron levels, as well as check on weight and the functioning of vital organs.

Initially, I also want to do a thorough evaluation of the person, to determine the best level of care for them. I'll determine, for example, whether a weekly visit with a counselor will be the most helpful to them, or two visits per week, or a more intensive level of care, such as a day hospital program, or if severe, a period of inpatient hospital treatment.

If meeting with a counselor as an outpatient seems an appropriate level of care, it is helpful to focus on what is happening at the emotional level for the person. I will further evaluate the level of depression. The person may need a medication consult with their doctor or a Christian psychiatrist. Sometimes medication (to treat depression) for a time can be very beneficial during the healing process. And I may encourage the person to have a nutrition consult with a registered dietician who works primarily with eating disorder patients.

I do not make a point of focusing on the eating habits themselves or on weight (in outpatient care). The focus is placed more on beginning to meet emotional needs and to help the person understand these needs.

What key areas do you focus on in the healing process?
Several key areas to focus on are:

- Individual worth/value (My favorite Scripture for this area is Psalm 139.)

- Being created with a purpose

- Relationship to God

- Evaluation of personal boundaries

- Developing helpful boundaries

- Nutrition, healthy eating, exercise as a lifestyle

- Development of support systems

What can family members and friends do to help?
Remember, it's not about food; it's about feelings! Be supportive. Keep lines of communication open. If you have a good relationship with this person, continue the relationship. You can gently encourage the person to eat out of concern for the person, but never try to force or be forceful about them eating. This will only make matters worse.

Respect the person as an individual. Respect their ideas and goals, even if they're different from your own. Sometimes this is difficult. Some very applicable sayings that come to mind are: "Don't sweat the small stuff" and "Pick your battles." As believers, it is helpful to prayerfully give the person over to our heavenly Father.

Eating disorders are definitely to be taken seriously; especially with a child or young teen, getting help is not optional—it's essential. Please be gentle with them, but definitive about how you are going to arrange help for them. With an older teen or an adult, your ability to influence them may be more limited. But you still want to gently and firmly express your concern for them and your expectation for them to obtain help. Let them know that you support them, will go with them, or will do whatever you can to see that they are helped.

APPENDIX B

RESOURCES

Organizations

- Overeaters Anonymous, www.overeatersanonymous.org; P.O. Box 44020, Rio Rancho, NM 87171-4020. Check your phone book for chapters in your area.

- The American Anorexia/Bulimia Association, Inc., 165 W. 46th Street, Suite 1108, New York, NY 10036; (212) 575-6200.

- National Eating Disorders Association, www.nationaleatingdisorders.org; 603 Stewart Street, Suite 803, Seattle, WA 98101; (206) 382-3587; Hotline (800) 931-2237.

- National Association of Anorexia Nervosa and Associated Disorders, anad.org; (847) 831-3438.

- The Renfrew Center, www.renfrewcenter.com; (800) REN-FREW. Centers are located around the eastern U.S.

- Focus on the Family, www.family.org, 8655 Explorer Drive, Colorado Springs, CO 80920; (800) A-FAMILY.

- Parent Talk *OnCall* Radio Ministry; www.flc.org/parent-talk/; P.O. Box 35300, Tucson, AZ 85740; (888) 888-1717.

- FamilyLife; www.familylife.com; 3900 N. Rodney Parham Road, Little Rock, AR 72212; (800) 404-5052.

Treatment Centers

- Minirth-Meier New Life Clinics, www.meiernewlifeclinics.com; (888) 7CLINIC. Refer to website or call to locate clinics in your area.

- Remuda Ranch, One East Apache Street, Wickenburg, AZ 85390; (800) 445-1900.

Books

- Dr. Neil T. Anderson, *The Bondage Breaker* (Eugene, OR: Harvest House, 2000).

- Dr. Neil T. Anderson and Rich Miller, *Reality Check: Winning the Mind Game* (Freedom in Christ 4 Teens series) (Eugene, OR: Harvest House, 1996).

- Shirley Brinkerhoff, *Nikki Sheridan Series* (Minneapolis, MN: Bethany House Publishers, 1996–2000). Book #4 is about eating disorders. All the books deal well with teen issues.

- Shannon Christian with Margaret Johnson, *The Very Private Matter of Anorexia Nervosa* (Grand Rapids, MI: Zondervan Books, 1986).

- Mary Jane Hamilton, *Living on Empty: How Intimacy with God and Others Transformed My Relationship with Food* (Wheaton, IL: Chariot Victor Books, 1994).

Resources

- Kimberly Kirberger, *No Body's Perfect* (New York: Scholastic Inc., 2003).

- Dr. Kevin Leman, *Bringing Up Kids Without Tearing Them Down* (Nashville, TN: Thomas Nelson Publishers, 1995).

- Max Lucado, *You Are Special: A Story for Everyone* (Wheaton, IL: Crossway Books, 2002).

- Cynthia Rowland McClure, *The Monster Within: Facing an Eating Disorder* (Grand Rapids, MI: Fleming H. Revell, 2002).

- Robert S. McGee, *The Search for Significance* (Nashville, TN: Thomas Nelson, 1998).

- Steve McVey, *A Divine Invitation* (Eugene, OR: Harvest House Publishers, 2002).

- Frank Minirth, et. al., *Love Hunger: Recovery from Food Addiction* (Nashville, TN: Thomas Nelson, 1990).

- Nancy Rue, *The Body Book: It's a God Thing!* (Grand Rapids, MI: Zondervan Books, 2000). (for preteen girls)

- Ruth Senter, *Longing for Love* (Minneapolis, MN: Bethany House Publishers, 1991).

- Patricia M. Stein and Barbara C. Unell, *Anorexia Nervosa: Finding the Life Line* (Minneapolis, MN: CompCare Publications, 1986).

- Alan D. Wright, *Lover of My Soul: Delighting in God's Passionate Love* (Sisters, OR: Multnomah Publishers, 1998).

Workbooks

- Stacey Kole, *Seeing Yourself Through God's Eyes* (Shannon Publishers, 2001).

- Andrea LoBue and Marsea Marcus, *The Don't Diet, Live-It! Workbook: Healing Food, Weight and Body Issues* (Carlsbad, CA: Gurze Designs & Book, 1999).

- Sharon Norfleet Sward, *You are More Than What You Weigh Handbook: Improve Your Self-esteem No Matter What Your Weight* (Denver: Wholesome Publishing Co., 1998).

APPENDIX C

WHO AM i?

To discover your true identity as a Christian, look up each of the following verses in the Bible and meditate on who you are in God's eyes. Reading one per day, in just over a month you can renew your self-image based on God's truth instead of the world's lies.

I am accepted...

John 1:12	I am God's child.
John 15:15	I am Christ's friend.
Rom. 5:1	I have been justified.
1 Cor. 6:17	I am united with the Lord, and I am one spirit with Him.
1 Cor. 6:19,20	I have been bought with a price. I belong to God.
1 Cor. 12:27	I am a member of Christ's body.
Eph. 1:1	I am a saint.
Eph. 1:5	I have been adopted as God's child.

Eph. 2:18	I have direct access to God through the Holy Spirit.
Col. 1:14	I have been redeemed and forgiven of all my sins.
Col. 2:10	I am complete in Christ.

I am secure...

Rom. 8:1,2	I am free forever from condemnation.
Rom. 8:28	I am assured that all things work together for good.
Rom. 8:31	I am free from any condemning charges against me.
Rom. 8:35	I cannot be separated from the love of God.
2 Cor. 1:21,22	I have been established, anointed, and sealed by God.
Col. 3:3	I am hidden with Christ in God.
Phil. 1:6	I am confident that the good work that God has begun in me will be perfected.
Phil. 3:20	I am a citizen of heaven.
2 Tim. 1:7	I have not been given a spirit of fear but of power, love, and a sound mind.
Heb. 4:16	I can find grace and mercy in time of need.
1 John 5:18	I am born of God, and the evil one cannot touch me.

I am significant...

Matt. 5:13,14	I am the salt and light of the earth.
John 15:1,5	I am a branch of the true vine, a channel of His life.
John 15:16	I have been chosen and appointed to bear fruit.
Acts 1:8	I am a personal witness of Christ's.

Who Am I?

1 Cor. 3:16	I am God's temple.
2 Cor. 5:17	I am a minister of reconciliation for God.
2 Cor. 6:1	I am God's co-worker (1 Cor. 3:9).
Eph. 2:6	I am seated with Christ in the heavenly realm.
Eph. 2:10	I am God's workmanship.
Eph. 3:12	I may approach God with freedom and confidence.
Phil. 4:13	I can do all things through Christ who strengthens me.

Reprinted from *Living Free in Christ* by Dr. Neil Anderson (Ventura, CA: Regal Books, 1993).

APPENDIX D

CONNECTiNG WiTH GOD

You were created with value and worth. Did you know...

1 God loves you and created you to know Him personally.
The Bible tells us...

God Created You
"You created every part of me and put me together in my mother's womb" (Psalm 139:13,14).

God Loves You
"God loved the world so much that He gave His only Son so that anyone who believes in Him shall not perish but have eternal life" (John 3:16).

God Purpose for You
[Christ is speaking] "My purpose is to give life in all its fullness" (John 10:10).

What keeps us from connecting with God and knowing Him personally?

2 Man is sinful and separated from God, so we cannot know Him personally or experience His love.

People Are Sinful

"All have sinned; all fall short of God's glorious standard" (Romans 3:23).

We were created to have a personal relationship with God, but by our own choice and self-will we have gone our own independent way and that relationship has been broken. This self-will, often seen as an attitude of active rebellion toward God or a lack of interest in Him, is an evidence of what the Bible calls sin.

People Are Separated

"The trouble is that your sins have cut you off from God" (Isaiah 59:2).

"The wages of sin is death" (Romans 6:23).

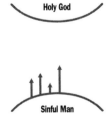

This picture illustrates that God is holy and people are sinful. A great gap separates the two. The arrows show that people are continually trying to reach God through their own efforts, such as a good life, philosophy, or religion—but they always fail.

What is the solution to our sin and separation from God?

3 Jesus Christ is God's only solution for our sin. Through Him alone we can know God personally and experience God's love.

He Died In Our Place

"God showed His great love for us by sending Christ to die for us while we were still sinners" (Romans 5:8).

He Rose from the Dead

"Christ died for our sins... He was buried, and He was raised from the dead on the third day... He was seen by Peter and then by the twelve apostles. After that He was seen by more than five hundred..." (1 Corinthians 15:3–6).

He Is the Only Way to God

"Jesus said to them, 'I am the way, the truth, and the life. No one comes to the Father except through Me'" (John 14:6).

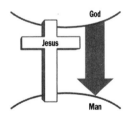

This picture illustrates how God has bridged the gap that separates us from Him by sending His Son, Jesus Christ, to die on the cross in our place to pay the penalty for our sins.

It is not enough just to know these facts about Jesus Christ...

4 We must personally receive Jesus Christ as our Savior and Lord; then we can know God personally and experience His love.

We Must Believe in and Receive Christ

"To all who received Him, He gave the right to become children of God. All they had to do was to trust [believe in] Him to save them" (John 1:12).

We Receive Christ by Faith

"It is by grace you have been saved, through faith, and this is not from yourselves, it is a gift of God—not by works so that no one can boast" (Ephesians 2:8,9).

When We Receive Christ, We Experience a New Birth
(See John 3:1–8.)

We Receive Christ by Personal Invitation

[Christ is speaking] "Behold, I stand at the door and knock. If anyone hears My voice and opens the door, I will come in to him" (Revelation 3:20).

Receiving Christ Involves:

- Recognizing our need for Christ
- Turning to Christ and away from self (repentance)
- Trusting Christ to come into our lives, forgive our sins, and make us what He wants us to be

Just to agree that Jesus Christ is the Son of God and that He died on the cross for our sins is not enough. Nor is it enough to have an emotional experience. We receive Jesus Christ by faith, as a decision of our will.

This illustration represents two types of lives:

Self-Directed Life
S – Self is on the throne
† – Christ is outside the life
● – Interests are directed by self, often
    resulting in discord and frustration

Christ-Directed Life
† – Christ is in the life and on the throne
S – Self is yielding to Christ
● – Interests are directed by Christ,
    resulting in harmony with God's plan

Which circle best represents your life?
Which circle would you like to have represent your life?

Here is how you can receive Christ:

You Can Receive Christ Right Now by Faith Through Prayer

Prayer is talking with God. God knows your heart and is not so concerned with your words as He is with the attitude of your heart. Here is a suggested prayer:

Lord Jesus, I need You. Thank You for dying on the cross in my place for my sins. I believe in You, and I open the door of my life and receive You as my Savior and Lord. Thank You for forgiving me of my sins and giving me eternal life. Take control of the throne of my life and make me the kind of person You want me to be.

Does this prayer express the desire of your heart?

If it does, pray this prayer right now, and Christ will come into your life, as He promised.

How to Know That Christ Is in Your Life

Did you receive Christ into your life? According to His promise in Revelation 3:20, where is Christ right now in relation to you? He said He would come into your life. Would He mislead you? How do you know He has answered your prayer? (You can trust God and His Word, the Bible. He will not deceive you.)

The Bible Promises Eternal Life to All Who Receive Christ

"Whoever has God's Son has life; whoever does not have His Son does not have life. I have written this to you who believe in the Son of God so that you may know you have eternal life" (1 John 5:12,13).

Thank God often that Christ is in your life and that He will never leave you (Hebrews 13:5). You have eternal life from the moment you receive Him.

Do Not Depend on Feelings

Our feelings about God and about what is true may change from time to time. However, the promises of God's Word, the Bible—not our feelings—is the basis of our confidence. The Christian lives by faith (trust) in God Himself and His Word. This train illustration shows the relationship among *fact* (God and His Word), *faith* (our trust in God and His Word), and *feeling* (which is the result of our faith and obedience).

The train will run with or without the caboose. However, it would be useless to attempt to pull the train by the caboose. In the same way, as Christians we do not depend on feelings or emotions to decide what is true, but we place our faith in the promises of His Word.

Now That You Have Trusted Christ

The moment you received Christ by faith, many things happened, including the following:

- Christ came into your life (Revelation 3:20; John 14:20).

- Your sins were forgiven (Colossians 1:14).

- You received eternal life (John 5:24).

- You became a child of God and a member of His family (John 1:12,13).

- As God's child you can now experience His special purpose and plan for your life (John 10:10; 2 Corinthians 5:17).

Wouldn't you like to stop and thank God for your new relationship with Him?

To enjoy your new relationship with God...

Connecting With God

How to Grow in Your Relationship with God

G Go to God in prayer. Talk to Him each day (Philippians 4:6,7).

R Read God's Word every day. It will build your faith (2 Timothy 3:16,17).

O Obey God when you know what is right (John 14:21).

W Witness—tell others about your faith in Christ, by your life and words (1 Peter 3:15,16).

T Trust God with every detail of your life (1 Peter 5:7).

H Holy Spirit—This is God's Spirit living in you. Allow Him to give you His power to live your life and tell others (Galatians 5:16; Acts 1:8).

END NOTES

Introduction

1. Julie K. L. Dam, "How Do I Look?" *People,* Sept. 4, 2000, p. 114.

2. Lindy Beam, "In Whose Image?" *Plugged In,* December 2000, p. 3.

3. Roni Cohen-Sandler, "Miss Perfect—Not!" *Girl's Life,* December/January 2001, p. 64.

Chapter Three: Facing What Is Real

1. Anna Quindlen, "Barbie at 35: Is She a Good Role Model for Youngsters?" *New York Times,* November 20, 1995, p. 4.

2. Ibid.

3. Ibid.

4. Lee Strobel, *What Jesus Would Say* (Grand Rapids, MI: Zondervan, 1994).

5. Elysa Gardner, "Britney's new show doesn't solve her identity crisis," *USA Today*, Nov. 9, 2001, p. E.01.

6. Carin Gorrell, "Sarah Ferguson: The Duchess Weighs In," *Psychology Today*, February 2002, p. 35.

7. D. Durham and P. Hanson, *Escaping Anorexia and Bulimia* (Colorado Springs, CO: Focus on the Family, 1992).

8. Dawson McAllister and Robert S. McGee, *Search for Significance: Youth Discussion Manual* (Nashville, TN: Word, 1990).

9. Nancy Thies Marshall and Pam Vredevelt, *Women Who Compete* (Grand Rapids, MI: Baker Book House, 1988).

10. *Search for Significance*, p. 71.

11. Ibid, p. 78.

12. Ibid, p. 79.

13. Ibid, p. 98.

14. Lindy Beam, "Teen Magazines and the New Feminism: How glossies look at sex, self-reliance, spirituality & more," *Plugged In*, April 2002, p. 4.

15. *NKJV Women's Bible* (Nashville, TN: Thomas Nelson, 1995), pp. 984, 1936.

Chapter Five: Healing for Life

1. "Cocoon of a Butterfly," India Campus Crusade for Christ brochure.

2. Carin Gorrell, "Sarah Ferguson: The Duchess Weighs In," *Psychology Today*, February 2002, p. 36.

3. Dr. Deborah Newman, *A Woman's Search for Worth* (Wheaton, IL: Tyndale House Publishers, 2002), p. 72.

4. Ibid., pp. 74,75.

OTHER BOOKS by NANCY WiLSON

Chosen With a Mission:
Are You Ready for the Adventure?

Delightfully entertaining, practical, and inspirational, *Chosen With a Mission* sizzles with Nancy's real-life adventures while presenting a solid blueprint for understanding and fulfilling the unique mission God has for each of us. You will discover possibilities of the Christian life from God's Word and His work in Nancy's life, such as:

- Her time behind bars, experiencing the true meaning of grace

- Her job as a dolphin trainer, learning that God's plan is never boring

- Her battle with an eating disorder, applying God's power to overcome

- Her world travels, practicing evangelism as a way of life

She seasons each story with insightful truth for readers of all ages. If you are ready for the adventure, *Chosen With a Mission* will get you started.

ISBN 1-57902-010-0

Chosen With a Mission:
Companion Study Guide
Ever wondered why you're here? Or what it means to be chosen by God?

Do you want to know God in a deeper way?

You will find answers to these questions and more as you work through the pages of this study guide. You will be challenged by thought-provoking questions, faith-strengthening truths from the Bible, and helpful encouragement for your prayer life.

Designed as a companion for Nancy's book *Chosen With a Mission*, this study guide can be used individually or with a group. The versatile content will benefit anyone interested in learning more about what it means to be chosen by God.

ISBN 1-57902-013-5

First Love: A Devotional
First Love captures the passion of an intimate relationship with Jesus Christ in a unique and moving fashion. Using the poems her father wrote for her mother during their courtship over fifty years ago, Nancy creatively parallels his expressions of love with the love our heavenly Bridegroom, Jesus Christ, has for His bride, the Church.

Nancy's poetry and intriguing devotionals give the reader a deeper understanding of the "bridal" love for Jesus. Her personal insights and scriptural principles will inflame your heart with a passion to respond to the Lover of your soul with fresh inspiration and commitment.

ISBN 1-56399-156-X

These and other fine products from *NewLife* Publications are available from your favorite bookseller or by calling (800) 235-7255 (within U.S.) or (407) 826-2145, or by visiting www.nlpdirect.com.

ABOUT THE AUTHOR

Nancy Wilson is a popular speaker for middle school, high school, and college students, as well as singles, women, and youth leaders. She also conducts prayer events and evangelistic outreaches. She speaks on a wide variety of topics, challenging participants to know and passionately pursue Jesus Christ and His mission for their lives.

To arrange for Nancy Wilson to speak at your event or for further information, contact her at:

100 Lake Hart Drive, Dept. 3200
Orlando, FL 32832
(407) 826-2174
nwilson@studentventure.com

If you're a student or parent who wants help in reaching others with the message of hope and God's love, check out **www.studentventure.com**. You'll find opportunities for growth, discipleship, conferences, etc.

For teens surfing the web, **www.beyondextreme.com** —"real life and what's beyond"—will help you explore real-life issues as well as spiritual interests.